W9-BBO-876

FIELDS OF LIGHT

Fields of Light

A Son Remembers His Heroic Father

PUSHCART PRESS
WAINSCOTT ■ NEW YORK 11975

Sponsoring Editors: Simon Michael Bessie, James Charlton, Peter
Davison, Jonathan Galassi, David Godine, Daniel Halpern, James
Laughlin, Seymour Lawrence, Starling Lawrence, Robie Macauley,
Joyce Carol Oates, Nan A. Talese, Faith Sale, Ted Solotaroff, Pat
Strachan, Thomas Wallace. Bill Henderson, Publisher.

Nominating Editor for this book: Andre Dubus

FOR MIRA AND JOSEF,
AND FOR CHRISTOPHER JAN AND HIS GENERATION.

ACKNOWLEDGMENTS

It was James Alan McPherson, my old friend and teacher, who gave me the original idea for this work, and Enid Thuermer made sure I discovered my spiritual home of Prague.

I am grateful, too, to those friends and family members who read over my many drafts of *Fields Of Light* and offered suggestions, including Lori Ambacher; Rachel Baldino; Katy Bedford; Carl Beckman; Tricia Butler; Debbie Chapel; Bethany and David Daniel; Susan Dodd; Bill Dorsey; Bill Goodman; Rob Grover; Morse Hamilton; Jack Herlihy; Ruth, Christopher, Mira and Josef Hurka; Beth Johnstone; Lisabeth Kirk; Dennis Lehane; George Macek; Lawrence Molnar; Ellen Nickel; Kristen Riley; Kate Roosevelt; Laurel Rushton; Carolyn Seymour; Jerry and Vicky Sperl; Hannah Turner; LuAnn Walther, and Carol Whitney.

Others helped with research, and/or kept me going with their good cheer: Nancy Alcorn, Donna Childs, Janet Loske and Marianne Savage at the Newburyport Public Library; Virginia Brereton; Connie Buzzell; Bill Cantwell; Andre Dubus III; Don Lee; Andrea McQuade; Art Norton; Jim Thomson, and Elissa Wald.

In the Czech Republic I was aided immensely by the Blecha, Hruba, Hurka, Moravcik, and Valta families, who took me in and gave me a home, and by Maruška Kublová, Jana Pazlarová, and Father Václav Malý. The Dubus family has always generously provided me with a second home on this side of the ocean.

Bill Henderson, of the Pushcart Press, offered me early hope and confidence in this project; he is a valued guide to me, and a rock of literary faith.

I gratefully acknowledge the kindness of Elizabeth Rea, who was so vital in helping these pages into print.

And Andre Dubus, in the stars, continues to make magic with his love. Thank you, Andre.

J.H.

CONTENTS

He that can endure
To follow with allegiance a fallen lord
Does conquer him that did his master conquer
And earns a place in the story.

William Shakespeare

FIELDS OF LIGHT

PROLOGUE

I am looking at a photograph of my grandfather with his two children. My father, probably age three, is angry because his mother has made him wear a hat. As a child my father resisted hats of any kind, and disliked being forced to do anything. His sister, Mira, is also unhappy because she has a cut on her knee and does not think she should be photographed this way. My grandfather seems to be displaying great patience and wisdom.

In leafing through family pictures, I find that Mira usually smiles, but my father rarely does. He seems to resent every attempt at primping for the camera and often scowls at the chore he's being put through. The family used to have fun with his moodiness. My grandmother would say that her boy Josef, or Pepa, could never hide his emotions—they were always clearly on his face.

The picture was taken around 1928, during a

heady era in Czechoslovakia. At the end of World War I the former Bohemian Kingdom, an oppressed subject for some three hundred years under the Habsburg Empire, had been liberated by Tomáš Masaryk and a group of Czech patriots. Slovak and Czech lands had been fused into a single republic. Masaryk, now president of the country, a brilliant scholar, philosopher and democrat, had brought in an unparalleled age of freedom and prosperity.

In another photograph, my grandmother stares out at the camera with hope and youth in her eyes. I think the picture was taken a few years earlier than the first, during my grandmother's teen-aged years. She was known then as Barbora Kublová. Everyone who knew her in her native Czech village of Žebrak, where she met and married my grandfather, has told me that she was a striking young woman. She was also a gifted actress who would eventually work in the National Theatre of Prague, some sixty kilometers northeast of her hometown. I met her only once, when I was a boy in America, not much older than my father in the first picture. She was in her sixties then, full of life and mischief, and as I write this and look at her eyes I can imagine how easily my grandfather must have fallen for her.

Her acting continued in community theatres after she and Josef, my grandfather, moved to a village near Žebrak called Radnice (pronounced Rad-*ni*-say). There, my grandfather owned a wholesale leather business and was the director of the Radnice bank and the family lived peacefully until 1938.

As my family stares at me from these photographs a hard future waits for them. For Tomáš Masaryk and his Republic were hated and feared by two men who were now planning the destiny of Europe, and Bohemia, dead in the heart of the continent, had always been an essential conquest for tyrants. Adolf Hitler would tear Czechoslovakia apart, and Joseph Stalin would enslave it, and under Communism Czechoslovakia would move into a forty-year night.

Then, two years after the Velvet Revolution, I would fly to the new Czech Republic to see precisely how my father and family fit into the time between that 1989 liberation and the moment, so long ago, when Mira worried about the cut on her knee and my father was unhappy about his hat.

CHAPTER ONE

COMING TO BOHEMIA

I flew toward Prague from Copenhagen on an SAS
Fokker 50, an older, smaller plane, though this morning
the weather over Europe was calm and the ride was
easy. Below my window, a patchwork of farmlands was
moving slowly by beneath sparse, drifting clouds. I did
not know what country I was over.

I shifted my right leg a little under the airplane
seat. I had broken it, just above the ankle, a few
months before, and the cast had just come off. The
thing was aching now, after a journey from Boston to
New York and New Jersey, then to Denmark and finally here.

There was a man sitting across the aisle from me,
and I had the feeling even before he spoke that he was
Czech, with his high cheekbones and china-blue eyes.
Then we met, and I told him Czechoslovakia was
where my father was from, and I was on my first journey to the Czech nation.

"I left in 1968," he told me.

"Where to?"

"Australia," he laughed. "They had work for a mechanic."

He handed me his card. *J. Pok*, it read. *Auto Electrical Service—Exchange Alternators, Generators, Starter Motors, Car Radios, Cassette Players and T.V. Repairs.*

"Looks great," I said.

"You must come and visit," Mr. Pok said. "Really. You must look me up if you come."

I told him I would. I liked his accent, the Czech-English, like my father's, but tinted with the Australian. He even said "mate" a few times. An attractive blond stewardess, coming up the aisle with her rolling table, somehow balancing everything in that small plane, handed him a coffee. He took it gingerly from her with his two hands.

"Nerve problem," he told me, showing me a scar on his wrist from an operation. "I'm crippled, but what the hell. I still can work. I always liked working. The Communists wouldn't let me do it because I never joined their comrades. That is why I left with my wife."

"My father wouldn't join them either," I said.

"When did your father leave?"

"In 1950."

"It wasn't a good time," Mr. Pok said. "I'm coming to see my brother and his family. It is the first time I have been back in twenty-five years."

We were both thoughtful a moment, looking out our windows at the green below. I shifted my leg a little again.

"You should tell your father to never come back," Mr. Pok said abruptly, and when I turned he was looking very directly at me. "The comrades ruined the country. It will never be the same as it was."

A stewardess announced that we were now over the Czech Republic and I looked down at that area that ancient history had known simply as Bohemia. All I could see was green and the contours of some hills. This was a land that I'd heard many stories about. Here my father and Mira had seen childhood. Here the Nazis had taken control after the capitulation of the British and French to Hitler at the Munich Conference of 1938, and my father had been put to work in one of their coal mines. Later, in 1949, when Czechoslovakia was under Communist rule, he had been imprisoned on a false charge of espionage. After surviving five Communist prisons he'd come out of jail determined to fight the Communist government, and had joined the Underground.

I did not tell my new friend any of this or that my father had no desire to see the land of his childhood again. My father had told me that he might return at some point only to visit Mira and pay his respects to his parents: beyond these, his connections with the nation he had fought for had ended long ago. He wished it well, but he was an American now, he said. At the same time, he was glad for me that I would be visiting the Czech Republic, glad that I could meet a side of my family which, during Communist times, I was not able to know.

And I wanted to see the country: perhaps I *needed* to: somewhere, in that land that drifted below me, a mystery was waiting for me that had to do with a heaviness and sorrow and pride I had felt all of my life, and that I was reminded of each time my father was disappointed by another human being, by a lack of honesty or an outright deception, each time he slipped into the strange depressions he is capable of and I tried to cheer him up with my spirit, to convince him that not all of humanity was bad. Things could get very black and white with my father, and during my teen-aged years when he ran his own engineering and consulting firm in Massachusetts and I acted as his helping hand, I sometimes gazed at his anger as if at a kind of void, wondering what made the storm suddenly blow. His anger was more mysterious because it was rare: usually he was quite even-tempered, and happy in the creative process of developing new products: the fiberglass ski and other revolutionary items for the ski and boating industries, winches for the European communications industry made of urethane and kevlar, tools and furniture molded from sawdust and fiberglass. Often, he spoke with great fondness about his boyhood, but his stories darkened and became sparse with detail when he approached his own teen-aged years, and prison, and his fight against the Communists, and I had never entirely pieced together his history from then on.

And Mira was down there, too, eager to show me Prague and the Czech Republic. During the few visits she had been allowed to the United States during Communist years, we had often hoped that I might have the chance to see Prague if the "Iron Curtain" ever lifted. My whole family had been nervous about my going there, the namesake of my father, while my father's enemies were still in power. But now Mira and I had been writing to each other for months, and I had asked to learn as much about the history of my Czech family as possible. She assured me she would show it all to me.

Our plane circled over Prague. Beyond the dipped wing, I saw the Strahov stadium, a gaping hole in the hazy metropolis, and the intercom stewardess told us that this was the largest stadium in the world. I looked over at Mr. Pok. The forefinger of his good hand was rubbing his lip, and his eyes kept switching from my window to the front of the plane. Then he turned to me again and said, "You must tell your father to never come back to this place."

Mr. Pok's hands shook horribly on the table when he presented his documents to the Czech customs official at Ruzyně airport. The country had not yet completed all of its uniform changes, and the customs official was still dressed in Communist green. Mr. Pok said to him: "I will talk to you in English. We must talk in English. I no longer speak my own language."

He was so agitated and shaking so much I was afraid he might have a nervous breakdown right there, and the customs official, a young man probably not over twenty-two, looked at him carefully. Then Mr. Pok seemed to gather himself together and his papers were approved and he was waved through. He waited for me on the other side of the iron turnstile for a while, but the customs officials had never seen a United States passport like mine, with a green cover, and I had to stand aside and let others go by while they checked me out. I waved to Mr. Pok and told him to go to his family. He clasped his hands with friendly defiance and smiled at me, and then he was gone.

It took them a full forty minutes to figure out that a green cover on a United States passport was the same as a blue one, and one of the customs officials, when he came briefly to the table, seemed quite hostile and distant. He was perhaps thirty-five and stood exceedingly straight-backed with his walkie-talkie close to his chest,

11

shaking his head at the passport and saying something to the effect that he didn't know what to make of it, giving it back to the younger man. The older man had hard, impassive eyes and glanced at me briefly and then left us and moved out through the line of waiting visitors as if they were trees. I guessed from his age and bearing that he was a former Communist, left now without a government to back up his arrogance. And I felt my anger rising, watching him and thinking of Mr. Pok and his reaction at the customs table; I had to calm myself by remembering that indeed, there was no real power left for such people. After my passport had made a tour of a back room, the younger official finally brought it back to me, apologized, and waved me through.

Mira was still waiting for me beyond the next set of doors, concerned at the time it had taken, and as we walked together out to the bus stop I explained to her about the passport. I said, "If I had wanted to somehow cheat, why would I have changed the color of my passport?" She told me, not for the last time, that many things still existed from the inefficient bureaucracy of the Communist age.

I looked at my aunt closely. Mira looked more healthy than I had expected: she was now seventy-one and had been having trouble with her hip. But her eyes were bright for me and she told me she couldn't believe I was there. She stood to my shoulders, her hair snow-white and carefully combed: she looked at me happily through glasses with colorful frames. I had the strange sensation of being intimately connected to a part of my family that I saw once only every few years. My aunt put her hand on my forearm, guiding me as we stepped across the drive.

I had strong memories of my time with Mira in Massachusetts and Illinois. She came first to visit my family when I was eleven, bearing a suitcase full of presents that smelled, when you unwrapped them, of a foreign world: chocolates and good luck charms and leather wallets and wooden sculptures and Bohemian glass and clothes. When I was older, I learned the terms under which she was required to return to Czechoslovakia: if she had requested asylum in the United States, her boss at the electronics firm where she worked in Prague would have been sent to prison. I began to understand that her visits were an extended leave from one large prison; I remembered now how, when my father came back from dropping her off at the airport, he would always have the same haunted look on his face, as if something terrible had just happened and he had been forced to simply watch and bear it. Vaguely, I had imagined what Czechoslovakia might be like from Mira and my father's descriptions: a land of spires and police and darkness, stained with this strange concept called Communism that followed Mira even to the United States, and that made people in her country talk freely to one another only in whispers.

So now Mira and I stood at the bus stop outside the airport. A few others gathered around us. The day was a little overcast, but it did not rain. Mira struggled some with her entry back into English, though she is quite good at the language when she has been able to speak it for a few days. I expressed regret that I knew no Czech. Ruzyně airport seemed quiet compared to airports in America, and very unlike my childhood imaginings of the country. The buildings were a little shabby, and the tar of the drive was cracked and worn. Occasionally, from behind the building complex we had just left, an airplane rose slowly and distantly into the sky.

The bus came up, an old and in some places rusting affair, and I hoisted my one suitcase aboard and sat with Mira and looked out at the gray day. We moved around an asphalt circle and then by what appeared to be another airport and Mira confirmed that that area, beyond cement and barbed-wire walls, had belonged to the Communists, and was now reserved for flights of government people and dignitaries. This construction, too, looked run-down, and I had the first thought of many this afternoon that I had stepped into a Third World country. Some grass grew wildly by the cement walls, and the sky was huge and gray beyond, and our bus rattled on.

Now we seemed to drive through a rural area for a time: some old, broken-down houses, some small neighborhoods, acres of grass growing untended. Mira asked me questions about my father—was he well? He *was* well, I confirmed, thinking this was not a lie, though Mira did not know that my father had been through a triple bypass in recent years and a number of other operations for his heart. He had asked me not to tell her this.

"He loves living in Vermont," I said, "because he is in the mountains."

"That's good," Mira said, nodding. "He always liked mountains."

She looked out the window. Even with her features smoothed by her relief in having me there, she had the same permanent sadness on her face that I had seen many years before, at a dinner once with friends in Madison, Wisconsin. I had been there with her and my father, and our hosts were Americans, and it had suddenly struck me how deeply sad, somehow, the faces of Mira and my father were, compared to the bright, unfettered features of our hosts. The sadness was characterized by an angle and set of the eyes, a length to the cheeks, as if their faces were preparing to apologize. You can feel a heaviness often too in the inflection of Czech voices: a hopeful rise at the beginning of sentences, followed by a dip at the end, the music of which seems to suggest an acceptance of fate. During my visit to the Czech Republic I was to find these things in the voices and faces of other older Czechs, and the beginning traces of them in the young as well. When the Czechs mean to be funny, such emotional gravity adds a slant on fate that makes their humor quite infectious: when they tell their history, it makes the listener still. When they point out your responsibility for something, which they do often, it makes their indictment of you maddening. And always, somehow, the demeanor of those Czechs I met, relatives and friends, seemed kind and forgiving.

Now we entered a more urban area, on the outskirts of Prague, walls and streets of stone, and gray, decaying, flat-roof style buildings that looked as if they might have been built twenty or thirty years ago. I stood up at one stop, for many people were getting on, and I wanted an older lady or man to have a seat: now, holding onto the metal bars above with many of the other people, and with Mira smiling at me and nodding her head in approval, I ducked my head again to look at the buildings as we went by them. Here was a row of gray apartments, with balconies on which tenants had strung-up laundry. The drying clothes hung straight this day. Some of the balcony floors, from this angle, looked as if they had been laminated with metal and wood, and the laminations were splitting apart. There were television satellite dishes on some of the balconies and roofs. I thought again of news documentaries of the Third World, and then of Harlem, and the Bronx, those parts of New York City I had passed through on my first leg of this journey, on a bus from Boston to New York's Port Authority station. There was one particular section of Harlem that had seemed, to me, to have been devastated by a war: blocks of nothing but broken fences, and glass, and tires, tenements blackened and falling apart, and everywhere, walls full of four-foot high graffiti reading *Crack Crack Crack*, as if in a kind of conquerer's bravado. This in front of me was a different kind of devastation, in these buildings and neighborhoods: it was more *interior*, somehow, and yet it still seemed as hopeless as the other. I pointed to the buildings and Mira said: "Apartments put up during Communist times. Aren't they terrible?"

"They're really in sad shape," I agreed. But soon the city was changing, and you felt you were entering a sophisticated urban area, old buildings sliding by that reminded me a bit of the brownstones you'll see in the older sections of Boston. We had made a couple of stops and there were many people crammed into the bus now, and at one point there was a screeching and halting of brakes and a tearing, metal sound—I wasn't sure what it was, but our bus seemed to be on its last legs—and a general alarm throughout marked by a chorus of high, concerned female voices. I was grateful to descend from the vehicle a few blocks later: a glimpse of buildings and people around us, and then steps to the subway, a lobby, and an escalator that moved us quickly down. It brought us to a clean, white and tile landing, a digital clock blinking numbers above

16

and train docks to either side. This was my first glance at the new, modern subway system that the Soviets had installed in the last few years of their reign, a network of spacious hallways and shopping centers and rounded shafts that trains whisked through. But now, between the language and the bold, attractive faces that flashed by me, and the crowds, I could not concentrate on much. I watched Mira's firm, small back before me, thankful for her guidance, and we made it to one of the platforms, and a train came quickly enough, and once we were on it it proceeded rapidly, taking us into the underground of Prague.

*   *   *

We ascended at a stop called Flora, a point I would soon be looking at on maps when I wanted to make my way back to Mira's apartment. Here the street was calmer, and I could take in more: more rows of buildings that looked like Boston brownstones, dark gray or sand-white in appearance, a fruit stand at the corner of Jičinská and Vinohradská with a poster of a shy, naked young woman that would become a kind of beacon for me: she adorned a fruit calendar, and her eyes and breasts showed, and then the calendar was hidden behind the window-ledge. There were some people sitting behind the fruit stand, having drinks at an outdoor bar, and above it the apartment buildings began, with shops on the ground floors.

In the distance behind us, rising above the city, was the local television tower, a strange, surreal structure that looked like a rocket from a nineteen-fifties B movie. Mira told me that many people in the Vinohradská, or Praha 3 district, had not wanted the new, democratic government to finish building the tower, which had been started by the Communists, because it aesthetically clashes with the rest of the area. But it was nearly done at the time of the revolution, and the government had decided to complete the project.

Revolution, I thought, and the thought excited me, of being within, now, a land that had reaffirmed its right to freedom and that had a playright, Václav Havel, at its helm. The young Czech women, with their high cheekbones and fierce good looks—these excited me, too: I had taken note of them on the bus, and in the subway as well. A few of them danced before my eyes again now, as we passed shops. There was a steady flow of people, primarily locals, in and out of these establishments. Many of the shops looked quite new: a grocery, a sports and weapons store advertising knives of different sizes and colors in the window, a small shoe shop, an elaborate office furniture supply store at the next corner with window displays of the gently-contoured desks and chairs and lamps of the day.

At 139 Vinohradská we stopped and Mira pulled out her keys and let us into her apartment building. Here was the address I had written to all of my life, and had never imagined I would see. It was a surprise that it could be an ordinary door into an unassuming apartment building. The entrance hall was dimly lit, and the tiles we walked over were old and cracked in the front hallway. Because of my suitcase, we took a lift to what Europeans call the first floor, or what we Americans would call the second floor. At that level there was a small foyer, a large window looking out onto a back park, and three doors. One of these was the entrance to Mira's apartment.

The building was built just before the Second World War, and Mira moved in soon after construction was finished. During those years she worked in a funeral home in the ancient area of Prague called the Old Town Square. Near the end of the war, she looked after my grandfather, who was in a city hospital with heart complications. He moved back to Radnice to live out his last days and died there in 1944. Then, as the Communists took a stranglehold on the country, and jailed my father as a political prisoner, life grew difficult for Mira and my grandmother. Former friends and neighbors turned their backs on them. Mira was denied the right to study law at Charles University and took a job as a technical draftswoman at the Tessla electronics firm in Prague, at half-pay. When she became sick with a kidney disease, my grandmother sold the Hůrka home in Radnice to pay for medical treatment and moved here, into Mira's flat. The Communists, who had released my father after holding him for eight months, now realized that he was working against them in the Underground. They turned their anger on the closest family he had left. Many nights the apartment was raided and Mira and my grandmother were questioned about my father's activities. They knew nothing: my father had cut off contact with them entirely, and that is probably what saved their lives. They lived together here, depending on one another, for nearly twenty years.

You enter what might be considered a foyer, perhaps nine feet wide and five feet deep. There is a single light above. There is, to your left, a toilet behind a curtain. In front of you there is a small refrigerator, not unlike those that students buy in the United States for college, and a set of shelves for foodstuffs. There are, in the short hallway, two standing closets which make the passage quite narrow.

The kitchen off this hallway doubles as a bathing

area, perhaps eight by nine feet. There is a small stove, a washer, a sink, a bathtub, and a window to an airshaft that smells distinctly of coal. Though there are no openings to daylight here, the light is bright, and the tiles of the floor are always clean, a shining, burnt-red color.

At the end of the hall is the only genuine room of the apartment, perhaps fifteen feet deep and some twelve wide. Here Mira has a couch that she sleeps on (you keep looking for a door to a bedroom, but there is none), a chair, and a dining table from the old homestead in Radnice. A glass case is set to the side for dishes, and Mira stores some old, family Bohemian crystal there; the walls have a few original paintings on them, also from my grandparents' home. By the couch there is a bookcase with photographs of my brother and me on the highest shelves. Everything is kept in careful order, but I had the feeling that a less organized person would have had great trouble living in a space this small, especially with another person—even someone as close as a mother—staying on for many years.

A window at the end of the room opens to Vinohradska Avenue, and a breeze from the street lifted the thin white curtains to greet me. I stepped over and brushed aside a curtain panel and looked down. I thought of how the Communist secret police (or StB, for "Státní Bezpečnost" in Czech) must have parked, just there, across the avenue in front of the bar, of how they had watched this place, had come into it at will and terrorized grandmother and Mira. And I thought of a news broadcast I'd seen two years before. It was a brief interview with Raisa Gorbachev, after the attempted coup in the former Soviet Union. She spoke of how terrifying it was to have someone break into their *dacha* and make prisoners of her and her family. And now my anger rose, at the window, as I thought that there could never be enough such nights to demonstrate to Raisa Gorbachev the kind of brutality that she, with all her self-assurance, espoused as long as she was on the right side of it. And I thought about how these few things, these pieces of furniture, these paintings and pieces of Bohemian glass, were all my family had left now.

And so when I called my father, ten minutes later, to tell him I had arrived, my mood was colored by the darkness of these thoughts and the memories of the neglected buildings I'd seen and the thought of Mira struggling for forty years. He sounded happy to hear my voice, and then quite concerned when I told him about the state of the buildings, and that "It's clear that this country has really been through something." I told him about my time with J. Pok, and about the man's advice that he not return.

I was not yet aware of how Prague, and this great, new and ancient country, was a place of physical and psychological contrasts.

Mira and I had a dinner of ham and rolls, and then went, a little later that night, to the Charles Bridge. I had seen it through childhood on many of her postcards: built originally in 1357 on sixteen pillars, and then with the addition of thirty statues during the seventeenth, eighteenth, and nineteenth centuries, the bridge is one of the most distinctive symbols of Prague.

But here was nothing I had seen on the postcards: a flow of people moving through the narrow, building-

21

encased streets toward the Old Town Bridge Tower. To our right, before the tower entrance, was a commotion and when we looked we saw four youths, drunk, dressed in black, held by two policemen. The police uniforms were different than those I'd seen at the airport, and Mira explained to me that these were the first uniforms changed by the democratic government— from the old green to a kind of blue outfit similar to that of American police. One of the youths, with a cornrow haircut, was sitting on a rock, loudly proclaiming something in Czech that everyone, including his friends, seemed to be ignoring.

"They have been drinking," Mira said, her voice lowered a little bit. "It's terrible. They look so stupid."

"It *is* kind of funny, though," I said, "the way nobody seems to be paying any attention to him." We chuckled about the drunk fellow and kept walking, following the V of the crowd moving toward the opening arch of the tower.

Now here was the entrance to the bridge, the Bridge Tower high above us, and youngsters playing tambourines and guitars beside us with other tambourines flipped over on the ground for money. Above, the statue of St. Vitus, patron saint of the bridge, and of Charles IV, the fourteenth century King of Bohemia and ruler of the Roman Empire and his son Wenceslas IV watched over us. Everywhere there were young people, faces of light and happiness, lovers, light and shadows playing over the cobblestones and the inner walls of the tower.

And then here we were, under and through the arch and into the open air, a crowd of people moving over the ancient bridge with us, more guitar players and groups of youngsters beneath the lamps, moths flying in that light, and now the night beyond clear and still, and a few stars were out. Below us, as we looked over the sandstone block walls of the bridge, ran the Vltava river. Lighted tour and dinner barges made their way downstream and you could hear the sounds of parties on board. The dark statues on the parapets stared down at me, Christ on His cross and saints and Good King Wenceslas, all of them, looking with the shadows on their faces, as if they were holding on to some ancient wisdom patiently in this loud, bright, cheerful night with the sounds of the young all around.

On the hill overlooking the city, Hradčany castle, the place of Bohemian kings, was lit now, white against the blue evening sky. St. Vitus cathedral, rising from the castle courtyard, seemed to stretch like a dagger toward the heavens. The flag of the president flew over the castle (it reads: *Truth Prevails*—a motto of the presidency since the time of Masaryk) indicating that Václav Havel was in Prague.

Later, at Mira's apartment, we prepared for sleep. Mira showed me how to fold her wooden chair into a platform, and we spread its thin cushion back on top of it. She gave me one white sheet and one large white comforter and one oversized pillow—these, I understood, were standard sleeping fare in the Czech Republic. For a time, looking at the thin chair cover, she tried to insist that she sleep there. I refused, but within two days I was using some extra back cushions from the couch to pad my bed. Thin mattress notwithstanding, I drifted into sleep that night quickly, having been up most of the past twenty-four hours. I occasionally woke to the traffic moving up Vinohradská and the electric tram going by, rolling thunder and bells, and to the sounds of that mysterious, strangely familiar language as people walked beneath our window.

In the morning I opened my eyes and saw the curtains stirring and heard the steady Vinohradská traffic, more routine-sounding somehow with the daylight, and my joints were quite stiff from my hard bed. I rose and did twenty push-ups and twenty sit-ups, these loosening me a bit, and resolved to do them each morning I was here. I took a bath and washed my hair and showered with a small, hand-held shower-nozzle that Mira has, and then, as we were preparing for the day, Mira brought out some things for me to have.

The first was the pocket-watch of my grandfather Josef, a Doxa made in France, now over eighty years in age. I turned it over in my hands, felt its heaviness. It was made of silver, with a simple design on its cover and underside, and the face of the clock was white, with ornate numbers giving European and military time. The watch was a little tarnished in places, but otherwise well taken care of, and I determined to have it looked at and cleaned when I got back stateside.

I held it with some reverence, this part of the everyday life of someone so important in my family. I would meet my grandfather later, at his gravesite in Radnice. He was apparently quite precise in his habits, and Mira said the watch was next to him, at his bedside, every night of his life, and that he carried it in the pocket of his suit every day.

Next Mira handed me a canvas satchel that used to belong to my father during his days at the military academy of Hranice, Moravia, the equivalent of West Point here in the United States. I realized that he must have used it during exercises in the field for tools and lunch. It was old and worn, and the original canvas straps had been, at some time, replaced with newer ones. As I turned it over and looked at it, I imagined it with my father on some trip through a forest, a simple reminder against his hip that there was one more meal there when he needed it.

Mira brought out a scout knife that my father once had, and a fork that he had acquired at some point during the war. The fork had the German eagle and reversed swastika engraved in its handle: it was dull silver in my hands, proof of what had happened here, in this place I'd traveled to.

And finally Mira had pictures, telling me that these and the other things were all mine to take, they were part of my "heritage," as she called it.

Here was my family, then. My grandfather in his leather shop, wearing his customary formal coat, and standing later in his life beneath the old tree at the Březina grounds, not far from Radnice, under which Goethe was said to create; my grandmother as a young woman, staring boldly back at the camera in a dashing summer hat. Here was Mira as a teen-ager, a bright-faced young woman in native Bohemian dress. And pictures of my father as a young boy, posing in another cap he hated, and in another photograph a rarity: a slight smile from him as he posed with some buddies, dressed in the traditional Sokol (a national sports and activities organization) outfit, shorts and shirt, leaning on a wooden rifle.

These were fascinating moments, this falling into years of my own blood. I stared for a long time at a picture of my grandfather with his gymnastics group, taken just before he went off to join the Austro-Hungarian army. In that morning light, as Mira went back to work in the kitchen, I slowly became a part of my family's story: I saw a fall day, light through trees, felt the flexing of muscles. *It was warm this day in the old town of Žebrak, but the leaves were falling from the trees and they skittered across the ground. On the outskirts of town, near the Hůrka home, my grandfather posed for the picture with five other friends from his Sokol sport group. He had just been recruited to fight for the Austro-Hungarian army, and his brother, Leo, had already left for the front. Perhaps he was thinking that he would send this photograph to his brother, as the photographer lined them up.*

I wondered how my grandfather felt about leaving the original Hůrka hometown of Žebrak and his family (a sizable group made up of his father and mother, one other brother, besides Leo, and two sisters). On the one hand, it was an honor to be drafted into the Austro-Hungarian army: on the other, not many Czechs were happy with the way they had been treated by the Habsburgs. I suspect my grandfather did not mind the thought of Barbora Kublová seeing him in uniform, though. On that day in 1914 he had probably been walking with her and courting her for some time. Looking at her picture, I imagined her blue eyes filling quickly with mirth, and that on their walks together she would push my grandfather's shoulder when he joked with her. He seems to have been formal and humble and with a shy, playful humor, and I have a feeling my future grandmother teased him mercilessly. I think my grandfather was very proud to have her.

Later, writing, I could see the two of them walking up to the ancient castle called Točník that looks over Žebrak on the afternoon after the gymnastics photograph was taken. I could see my grandmother, young and flushed with color, looking out over the town and the hills of Bohemia and my grandfather watching her profile quietly.

Then he was on the front in Hungary. I saw him running hard where twilight and the light of explosions flickered through trees. I saw him gripping his rifle and out of breath from the running and the weight on his back. Others were running around him, and there was confusion there, for the tide of the battle was turning and he saw men going in the opposite direction. Then there was a white flash and for a moment he was running in air: he came to a minute later and the smell of the ground was stunningly fresh and close to his face and he tasted metal in his mouth and two sets of hands were grappling with his shoulders, pulling him up, and a voice close to him said Can you run and Josef said Yes and he was running with their help; it didn't matter how much his leg hurt him, if he stayed there he would never run again.

He recovered during a late summer in Szolnok, Hungary, and soon he was well enough to walk. He went to a photography studio in town that did a booming business in postcards with all of the wounded soldiers coming through. The postcard was here, in the stack of photographs Mira had given me. I turned it over. On the back of it, in August of 1915, my grandfather had written: *Darling—Many regards and kisses. Yesterday, a friend brought pictures from a photographer and I am sending you one. My uniform is a bit crumpled but it is not my fault—apparently the photographer's "hot iron" was too cold, don't you think? When am I going to get yours? Greetings and kisses. Pepa.* He wrote down my grandmother's address, and above it his own: *Hůrka, Group 5—288 Marsh Company, Hungary.*

His older brother, Leo, always the one to watch out for the rest of the Hůrka children, had managed to secure a job in Poland acquiring livestock and other supplies for the troops, and he evidently found a way to have both of his brothers, Josef and František, serve also in this way. It was safe work and would provide a basis for the brothers' future careers: Leo would become a wealthy man, trading cattle after the war, and Josef and František would be involved in related businesses.

Very few Czech soldiers had their hearts in the war—many in fact deserted and joined the other side. As I write this and look again at the postcard I think that perhaps my grandfather, staring into the camera, momentarily dreamed of Žebrak: of what it would be like to descend from the bus in the square and walk through the alley to the back road that led to the Hůrka home: there would be roosters cackling and rabbits snuffling in the gardens behind the buildings, and perhaps it would be evening. And the most delightful decision for him, carrying his rucksack and hardly believing he was there, would be whether to visit Barbora or his family first.

After their marriage in Žebrak, Josef and Barbora moved to nearby Radnice, a small village which on maps shows up nearly in the exact center of Europe. By then, Leo was already operating his successful livestock business in Prague, and my grandfather started his own business, doing wholesale trade in leather and developing patterns for leather products. In October of 1921 Mira was born, and in August of 1925 my father after her. The young family settled into a productive, easy life, and as my father and Mira grew much was changing for the better in the newly-liberated nation called Czechoslovakia.

Grandfather Josef with his two children: Josef (left),
and Mira, about 1928.

CHAPTER TWO

ANCIENT VOICES

Ancient Bohemia is a place of kings and mythical heroes and beauty and war and intrigue. It is the home of Princess Libuše, the leader of a female-dominated Slavic tribe who first envisioned Prague and gave birth to the Přemyslid dynasty in the seventh century; of Good King Wenceslas, the Přemyslid ruler who was assassinated by agents of his brother Boleslav in 935; of Charles of the House of Luxemburg, the fourteenth-century king of Bohemia and Emperor of Rome who made Prague his political center and ruled over its golden age. Under the hand of Charles, during a time of bold architecture and construction, rose distinct symbols of the Czech nation: Charles bridge and Charles University, and the king's towering castle in the countryside, Karlštejn.

Such were the tales of history told to Mira and young Josef as children. Their parents, both avid readers, were always reading to them or telling them the stories, and history was all around them: the walls of little Radnice had stood for centuries, and had witnessed knights and nobles, and three hundred years of resistance to the Habsburgs. It was in Radnice, in fact, that the eighteenth-century priest A. J. Puchmajer first organized a Czech reading club—a direct violation of an order by the Austro-Hungarian Emperor banning Czech as an official language. A network of such clubs grew into a quiet but determined nationalistic movement, and kept Czech culture alive through the darkest Habsburg years.

By the onion-steepled church that Puchmajer served in, standing on the town square, was the statue of Jan Hus. It had been put up a few years before my father's birth, sculpted for the Bohemian priest who, in 1415, had died at the stake for his opposition to a corrupt Germanic-Catholic papacy. Sometimes, the children would watch Hus' silent face against a backdrop of trees, wondering what it would have been like to live in his time, and to meet him. Their parents spoke of the martyr's allegiance to the truth—the new president, Masaryk, they said, was like another Hus in his love of truth.

Each evening of July 6, on the date of the Jan Hus' death, Mira and Josef and their friends gathered to watch the hills above Radnice, where bonfires flickered in honor of the ancient Czech priest.

The children, too, were living in an historic time, though they were not as aware of it. Tomáš Garrigue Masaryk had established the first democracy that central Europe had ever known. During the war he had traveled through Europe, Russia, and the United States promoting the independence of Czech and Slovak lands. He had been given strong support by America and Britain, and by a fierce resistance to the Habsburgs on the homefront. His vision was of a government based largely on the American experiment, and he had actually signed the Czechoslovak Declaration of Independence on October 26, 1918, in Independence Hall, Philadelphia.

Masaryk, nearing seventy when he took office that year, brought a lifetime of scholarly and practical experience to his work. He had served in the Vienna Parliament, and worked as a professor of philosophy for many years in the Czech University of Prague. He was an author, spoke seven languages, and was considered by friend and foe a rock of integrity. As president Masaryk had secured rights for citizens that were years ahead of their time: a health-insurance fund (to which employees and employers contributed equally) that guaranteed medical treatment to all workers and their families; paid sick or pregnancy leave for up to fifty-two weeks, and guaranteed education. Minority groups were given fair representation in the National Assembly. Business was brisk and profitable in Masaryk's Czechoslovakia.

My aunt and my father's memories of this time seem to be simple ones. Later in my trip, I would see the places of their formative years, the streets of Radnice where they played and the hills surrounding the village where they hiked and skied. I would walk up on Kalvárie (Calvary), the hill with a small chapel that, dressed in their finest outfits, the children went up to each Easter Sunday. I would ride the train that they took to "gymnasium" and see that school, stepping through its hallways and thinking of the busy shouts of the youngsters as they arrived in the morning. And so, writing later, I could see moments of their childhoods as they had told them to me.

I could imagine, for instance, Mira and my father as youngsters on a winter day; an old farmer came to a field outside Radnice with his horses and sleigh, and the town children would climb aboard, and those who could not fit in the sleigh would be connected to it by rope on their own sleds, like a trail of sausages. The farmer took them around and around the snowy field, and my grandmother and grandfather watched with other parents, cheering.

The town closed off steep Kalvárie street nearby for sledding and once young Josef, aged five, piloted his sled with his friends Venca Karlíček, Vláďa Nachtman and Zdeněk Blecha in back, and at a sharp turn ran them all into a fence: the pilot wound up hanging on a fence-post by his chin, facing an afternoon of stitches.

In family stories about my father there is a clear, steady thread of self-generated trouble running through his young life. There is a scene after school one day, for instance, when Josef and a friend were serving "guard duty" at Christ's grave—a smooth block of granite in the Radnice church. They set up books on the tomb for a net and, pulling ping-pong paddles and balls from their rucksacks, launched into a serious game to pass the time. Their priest, discovering this sacrilege, lifted both of them by their collars and, without saying a word to either, put them firmly down on the outdoor step.

To young Josef's horror, his mother often dragged him to her acting performances in Rokycany and sometimes put him up on stage with her as an extra. It made him miserable to stand in front of all those people. But in the winter afternoons he could escape school work and the theatre with his skiing: at first it was in the hills surrounding Radnice, and then in the Šumava and Gross Arbor mountains to the south with his Sokol group, where he won his first races. Somehow on the snow, in the long, sweeping turns between the blue and red-colored gates, he could forget everything. He enjoyed the breadth of the mountains on the horizon and the crisp, sunlit days. He liked the speed, the feeling of the white slope dropping beneath him.

As he grew older, Josef was constantly on motorcycles, an early love. His best friend, Zdeněk Blecha, had a father who owned a machine shop, and the boys spent hours tinkering with the bikes there: they played soccer on them in the nearby fields and rode them fast through trails in the woods. One of my father's strongest memories is of an early teen-aged birthday when my grandfather walked with him to the Blecha garage and there, with Zdeněk and Mr. and Mrs. Blecha smiling and watching him, he saw for the first time his very own, gleaming new ČZ Česká Zbrojovka motorcycle.

Mira's chief difficulty seems to have been in chaperoning her younger brother. She was a good student at the Rokycany school, and my father was as well, when he put his mind to it. But because Mira was older, her teachers held her responsible for Josef when he got into mischief. And that was often. It was difficult for Mira to keep track of him, for they walked in separate groups to the Radnice train station in the mornings, and the boys and girls rode in separate train cars. And so once, when professor Velíšek approached Mira and said he was sorry Josef had been sick for so long with a contagious disease and needed to be quarantined, Mira had difficulty finding a response. It had been nearly two weeks now, the teacher said and, by the way, if she was living in the same house, why wasn't she, too, quarantined?

After school Mira marched to the area in the hills around Radnice that she knew her brother had a liking for. She found him there, with Sprnda Spěváček, Zdeněk Fajta, and Jarda Čermák, *sunbathing* on some rocks near a cave. She gave them such a fierce talking-to that my father still drops his head a little in shame when he is reminded of it. For a time, on the bargain that she not tell her parents, Mira made him report to her in-between periods to make sure he was attending classes.

"If I did not love him so much," Mira told me, on one of our May nights together in Prague, "I would have killed him."

On Wednesdays, Fridays, and on the weekends there were movies at the Sokolovna, the same gym where the Sokol groups met for athletics, and there in the darkness the children saw films from all around the world. Josef liked the American films that followed tales he had read with his father, like *Mutiny on the Bounty* with Clark Gable and *Captain's Courageous*, Mr. Kipling's story, starring Spencer Tracy. He liked Marlene Dietrich and Gary Cooper too, though that movie about how she stole a necklace and slipped it into Gary Cooper's pocket, *Desire*, was a little heavy on the romance for his taste. He liked the Marx Brothers' films, the pretty skating star Sonja Henie, and the shoot-'em-ups with the gangsters.

Just before the features came on there were the ten-minute newsreels, and at age twelve Josef watched the pictures of the fighting in Spain, of Franco and

Hitler, of the German planes storming across Spanish skies. Not all of this meant much to him, of course, but he had noticed that the adults were beginning to talk and argue about the news a great deal. One night he overheard two older men, in back of the movie house when he left, talking about Adolf Hitler's book *Mein Kampf*.

"I'm telling you," one of these men said. "He's going to wipe out you Jews. He wants to build an empire all the way to Russia, and turn us all into his slaves."

"He won't have a chance," the second man said, laughing. "We Jews will pave the way to his heart with gold."

Many of Josef's afternoons were spent in that same Sokol gymnasium, the movie equipment and chairs cleared away, and the men and teen-agers—boys and girls—practicing on the gymnastics equipment. In fall you played soccer, in winter you skied or skated, and in summer the Sokol organization brought the children on camping and hiking trips. And select groups—Josef's Radnice group was one of them—were chosen to perform once every six years with thousands of other Sokol members in colorful athletic displays in Prague's Strahov stadium. In 1938, Josef and the Radnice group demonstrated their proficiency at the Sokol festival with wooden rifles, spinning and handling them smartly. The vast audience, cheering for the twenty-thousand performers, were overwhelming in their enthusiasm. For the gymnastics demonstration was more, this year, than a festival. It was an expression of national unity in a world fast closing in on the small country.

Josef had also recently joined the Boy Scouts, and spent many days in the same wide-hat and brown uniform worn by many American boys of the time. His troop took a number of camping and canoeing trips on the Berounka river near Radnice, and he loved guiding a canoe through a "V" sluice of white rapids, then looking up when you got to the quiet water, at the pine forest that lined the river and the occasional castles on the cliffs.

More and more, in 1937 and 1938, his scout troop was being trained in civil defense. At the elementary school near the church in Radnice, in the evenings, the boys were taught first-aid by town doctors. But Josef was more impressed with the air-raid exercises that his troop was involved in: high on Kalvárie hill, imagining that German planes were coming in the same way that they did in those newsreels, he would signal the town below in Morse code with large signal flags. If war ever came, he hoped he would have this job. It was important, and he could imagine sending his signal and hearing the air-raid sirens start. As he walked home after scouts, thinking of all this, he crossed the bridge into the žamostí or "quarter behind the bridge" area of town, where the municipal bulletin board was filled with patriotic slogans and posters.

When President Masaryk died in 1937, Josef went with his troop to participate in the funeral in Prague. There, in St. Wenceslas Square, he saw the funeral cortege of the great man roll by him, escorted by horses, their hoof-beats echoing steadily through the crowded, hushed avenue.

Masaryk had resigned his office two years before, at the age of eighty-five, and now he was gone. He had served his country as its visionary, egalitarian leader for seventeen years, and to this writer it seems a blessing that he did not live to see all that would happen to his country.

But he had long foreseen the danger represented by the German state to the west. In an article published in 1916, while Masaryk was in England, the future Czech president had written: *"The programme of the Allies...must be a plan of defense, a plan for promoting the moral and political progress of Europe and of Humanity. (It must) force Germany to be human, to accept and to comprehend the humanitarian programme of the best German thinkers. Germany, when she has abandoned the ferocious philosophy of the superman and the policy of the 'blond beast' aspiring to the bloodstained dominion of mankind, will easily find her place as an equal among equals."*

Into Masaryk's place had stepped his close friend and former student, the Czech minister of foreign affairs, Dr. Edvard Beneš. The new president was immediately faced with the relentless military ambition of Adolf Hitler. But Czech fortifications, mostly concentrated in that area bordering Germany called the Sudetenland, were strong, and at Beneš' word, eight hundred-thousand Czechs could be mobilized to fight the Germans.

There is a formal portrait of President Beneš in a 1937 military promotional booklet that Mira gave me from this time. The booklet had been passed out in the Boy Scouts to my father: young Josef was apparently already dreaming of serving in the Czech Air Force. Next to the Beneš picture is a patriotic message from the president to the young men of the country, and the book's pages are filled with colorful depictions of various Czech uniforms; I imagine my father looking with longing at the officer's cap he would wear one day—

green, with the crown of the Bohemian lion and golden braid around the rim. There is a small fold-out map of the *Republika Československá*. There is a page of symbols of other armed services in Europe: perhaps Josef wondered about the strange symbol next to *Německo*, *Finsko*, and *Lotyšsko*, Germany, Finland, and Latvinia, the odd twisted cross like a black spider, spinning counter-clockwise with bending legs—where did the Germans dream it up? In the back of the book, in pencil, twelve year-old Josef Hurka drew a gun firing and a precise rendering of the Czech flag.

*   *   *

Almost seven hundred years before my father worked on his sketches, Bohemian King Přemysl Ottokar II invited Germans to settle with Slavs in the Bohemian Kingdom. German settlers moved into the mountains in the west of the Czech lands, into what would later be called the Sudeten forest. The new settlers were more proficient at farming and mining than their hosts, and there was friction. The region quickly became a hotbed of conflict between the two nationalities, and their anger at one another grew to span centuries.

Now in 1937 Adolf Hitler was listening to his own version of these ancient voices. And Czechoslovakia, home of the hated Slavs, stood in the way of his true goal: *lebensraum* (living space) in the east—the conquest of Russia. To have Russia, his troops would need to sweep across Bohemia: to have satisfaction, he would see the Czechs, one day, as the slaves of his thousand-year Reich.

The German Fuehrer, fresh and emboldened from his takeover of the Austrian government, fixed his sights first on the Sudetenland. An ancient home of

Germans, wrongly delegated to the artificial Czech state at the end of World War I, he argued, was by rights part of Germany. He was aided by the Sudeten German party, (SDP) which clamored for the favored status Germans had enjoyed under the Habsburgs.

Czech fortifications in the Sudetenland and the strength of the Czech military were, for the Western Allies, a last opportunity to stop Hitler. But British Prime Minister Neville Chamberlain, unlike the man who would soon replace him, Winston Churchill, had no such vision. Chamberlain's main concern in 1937–38 was in finding a way to placate the angry dictator of Germany. If it was part of a small country Hitler wanted, why not secure it for him to avoid war? Hitler had, after all, promised that after this conquest he would have no more territorial demands in Europe.

During negotiations at Munich in the autumn of 1938, as Chamberlain fed Czechoslovakia to Hitler, Edvard Beneš mobilized Czech forces. My father remembers this time: my grandfather, Mr. Blecha and all of the other men of Radnice pulled out their uniforms and prepared to go to the front. Large, brand-new military trucks rumbled by the Hůrka home, "running-in" the engines. My grandmother was worried about the bloodshed to come: my grandfather, like most of the men, was furious at Hitler's audacity and eager to fight for his nation.

Josef and Mira followed what happened to their country then with growing dismay, sitting in the living room at 145 Švehlova with their parents, listening to a Philips radio: Czech announcers reported that Chamberlain was demanding the demobilization of Czech troops; the Prime Minister said that if war came to Europe, the Czechs would be solely responsible. Other allies, France and Poland and Romania—all of which had mutual protection assurances with Czechoslovakia—deserted the Czech nation now as well. Josef and Mira watched the troubled pacing of their father when Beneš, faced with the opposition of his allies, finally surrendered the Sudetenland. "It is terrible," father Hůrka said, sinking into his chair, his eyes looking far beyond the walls of his home. "Don't they see what will happen? Terrible."

It was September 30, 1938. At five o'clock that evening, Czech Premier Syrový announced on Czechoslovak Radio: "We were abandoned. We stand alone." The official announcement of the Czech government was that Czechoslovakia had given up the vital Sudetenland "under protest to the world."

At the Nuremberg trials seven years later German General Keitel would admit: "We were extraordinarily happy that (the Sudetenland occupation) had not come to a military operation . . . From a purely military point of view we lacked the means for an attack which involved the piercing of the frontier fortifications (of Czechoslovakia)."

Without the "Czech Maginot Line," as the Sudeten fortifications were called, and without the industrial strength of the Sudetenland, Czechoslovakia now lay at the mercy of Germany. Czech democratic leaders had no doubt about Hitler's intentions. Within the month of the Sudetenland occupation President Beneš resigned, traveling first to the United States and settling eventually in London, where he set up a Czech government in exile. He was soon followed by his chief of Intelligence, Frantisek Moravec, who came to Britain with eleven of his most trusted aides. The heads of the Czech Intelligence community left swiftly on the night of 13 March, 1939.

Two days later, facing no resistance whatsoever, and violating all of Hitler's assurances to the contrary, the Nazis rolled into Prague.

*   *   *

As the world was embroiled in the Munich crisis, my father was trying to deal with the problem of Ada Vostrý. Ada was the oversized son of a butcher who happily tormented all children in Radnice smaller than himself. He held a special wrath for Josef, who had, during a sand-skiing trip in the last week of summer, shot him in the ass as he was bending over to tie his bindings. Thirteen year-old Josef ran so fast that time that he left the gun right there, and Ada had been unable to catch him. The problem for the bully was that it had happened in front of just about everyone.

Day after day, when the boys came off the train from school, Ada chased Josef. Day after day, when Josef walked in the village, he avoided the places where Ada was supposed to be. The ducking and running went on for weeks.

And then finally, one day when Josef had had enough, he waited in a field just a short walk down from the train stop. When the older boy came lumbering at him, full of his hate, something in Josef went black. He swung his fists hard at that surprised face and beat the butcher's son senseless. The other boys stood around, stunned and quiet at this show of sudden fury.

That March, as the Nazis invaded the rest of the country, Josef and his friends walked to the Rokycany school after getting off the train. And there in the main highway sat a German tank. The boys went over to it and kicked the iron solid tread defiantly, and the soldiers in the turret above them laughed.

The German regular (Wehrmacht) soldiers were generally cordial to Czech citizens at first, and happy that their marks, set by the Nazis at an absurd ratio to the Czech crown, bought them so much. In stores, the youngsters noticed, Czech adults usually treated their Nazi occupiers with disdain. For a time the Czech nation, though living under a shadow, seemed to move through its normal routine. Many of the usual functions of the government, such as school and Sokol activities, continued on. But it was odd to constantly see the Nazi soldiers; they stood at street corners with submachine guns slung over their shoulders, or drove through town on motorcycles with side-cars, looking always *through you* as they passed—through these Czechs that were only a phase in their plan.

At Sokol camp that following summer, an SS man walked into the pool area where Josef was swimming. Apparently, the man was a friend of one of the lifeguards. Josef was impressed when the black-uniformed soldier, gripping the handles of the pool ladder, raised himself into a rigid handstand. To Josef, trained in Sokol gymnastics, it was an impressive feat.

Then the war began, and things grew dark quickly in Czechoslovakia. The Nazis, even regular Wehrmacht soldiers, grew brisk and impatient with the locals. The bulletin board near the end of the bridge, long cleared of patriotic posters and slogans, now was filled with a listing of the locals who had been "executed for high treason." Jews packed their bags and, told they were being brought to eastern internment camps, were never seen again.

It soon became clear that the Czech Jewish population was in desperate trouble. Members of the Resistance in Rokycany asked youngsters, including Josef and his friends, to scout out the caves in the area, so that the Resistance could pull the Jews off the trains heading toward Terezín and hide them. This the boys did easily, as many of the caves had been their haunts when they had skipped classes.

Throughout the country there was a strict evening curfew: all exterior lights out at nine o'clock. Shortwave radios were required to have their short-wave circuits removed, under punishment of death. Mr. Blecha, however, devised a solution: a circuit that one could plug in and out, as needed. With it, Josef and his family gathered around the Philips radio in the evenings to hear the BBC European News Service broadcast from London. Often Jan Masaryk, son of the late president and the former ambassador to England, spoke to darkened Europe with his strong, determined voice. "The German murderers should remember this," he said, during one broadcast. "Truth is bound to win in the end, and one of these days their Axis will stop turning. It is a very difficult task for civilized people to perform, but it is sacred and very, very necessary."

At night, in Radnice, Josef and Zdeněk still rode their motorcycles sometimes, using illegal fuel. But mostly their night hours were for errands: Josef made many trips over the dark rural roads on a bicycle to get milk and eggs from a farm nearby for his family, his shadow scalloping over the tar in the moonlight. A violation of the war curfew and rationing could bring trouble, but if you got stopped, as Josef did once, it was usually by Czech police, and they let you go.

One morning in 1941, the head of the Rokycany school, Dr. Horak, met with the students in a general assembly. He spoke frankly with them. He had just come from a meeting with Nazi officials in Prague, he said, and it was imperative that the students not get involved in any anti-Nazi provocation: otherwise their school would be closed down. The Nazis had told him that they did not care one way or the other if Czech children received higher educations. *If we lose the war,* Dr. Horak quoted them as saying, *you can set up your own schools again. But if we win, your children will require only a third-grade education to serve us.*

The whole country had felt or seen the horror of Nazi methods toward Czech education by then, of course. Mira lived in Prague now, and Josef often worried about her. She had gone to Charles University to study law. But after a student protest in October of 1939 the Nazis had taken the leaders of the student council to Ruzyně airport and murdered them before a firing squad. Other student residences in Prague had been invaded one night soon after, and the students who resisted were beaten, arrested or shot. One thousand Prague students had been seized and brought to the Oranienburg concentration camp, where they were still being held hostage to insure "good behavior" on the part of other Czechs. Soon after that bloody October, all Czech universities had been closed and Mira had taken a job keeping books in a funeral home in Prague. Her former law school was now an SS barracks.

And now SS General Reinhard Heydrich, Hitler's

newly-installed 'Reichsprotektor of Bohemia-Moravia,' instituted his compulsory youth service under which youth in the Czech lands would work for the *totaleinzatz*, the total war effort. Those born in 1924 or before were shipped to Germany to provide labor for factories: Josef had been born in 1925 and would be put to work at home. Secretly, Heydrich had decided that this effort would pull children away from their Czech teachers, a first step in "Germanizing" them. Those who could not be Germanized (Heydrich had determined—somehow—that this would be between forty and sixty percent) would be exterminated with the Jews.

But Josef, now sixteen, had no interest in working for the German war effort. Told he was going to be brought daily to a foundry in Vranov, near Radnice, he dodged the work crew. The Nazi police picked him up and drove with him toward Prague.

There, Mira and her uncle Leo got a call from the family that Josef was in trouble. They drove to the Gestapo office on Vinohradská just in time to see Josef sitting defiantly in chains on the back of the Gestapo truck as it pulled in.

"Big hero," Leo said, shaking his head. And after Leo had bribed a Nazi guard with a large salami to let the boy go, he gave his nephew a long talking-to. "These fellows aren't playing games, Pepa," Leo told Josef.

School during those years was run only at the behest of the Nazis, and during long stretches in the winter and summer when it was closed, Josef worked. At first he screwed together small irons at the foundry. Then, after a brief time, he was moved to a coal mine nearby, in Chomle. It was a shaft-mine, over one-thousand feet below the earth, and the work was dangerous and primitive: recently, at a mine next door, one hundred and forty men had drowned when a new shaft had been cut too close to an older, flooded one. The mining was back-breaking; after dynamite had broken open a new underground area, Josef's job was to go in with his shift and shovel the coal into railcars, eight hours a day steadily with a short break for lunch.

But there was a way to get back at the Germans. At Rokycany, two friends of Josef's from school approached him, saying the Resistance needed dynamite. After the dynamite crews had left a newly-cleared area in the mine, they would leave fresh dynamite sticks in a pile for the next clearing crew. Someone from the Resistance would always leave a little more than needed. Josef, for the two years that he worked the mines, would quickly tape the extra explosives to his legs, under his pants, and work like that until the end of the day when he went up the elevator and by the guards. Though there were random searches of the miners, he was never caught. In Radnice, he left the dynamite beneath a tree on the hill called Florian, to the southeast of the town.

He never told anyone about stealing the explosives.

I imagine my grandfather now, as I write. He is walking through Wilson train station in Prague on a December evening in 1941. It is a long time since he walked in Žebrak with my grandmother and she pushed his shoulder, joking with him. His footsteps echo on the tiled floor.

Today, he has visited Leo in the Little Quarter: from Leo's windows looking onto snowy Nerudova street they have watched German SS officers casually greeting one another in front of a cafe. These men smiled and conversed, holding themselves very straight, their Walther pistols strapped to their waists. One threw back his head in laughter at something said by another. They spoke with one another as if the Czechs, moving sullenly and quickly by them, did not exist. They are all over the city, these black-uniformed, proud minions of Heydrich and Hitler.

My grandfather sits on one of the benches in the center of the hallway. He needs the rest, for he has walked a great deal today. In his gloved hands is a cane, and he lays it across his lap. He puts his hat on the bench beside him. He stares at the hat, feeling a little dizzy, and then the feeling passes and he pulls out his Doxa watch. Twenty minutes until his train to Plsen arrives. An announcement comes through the hall: a train is coming in at one of the docks outside.

A few other commuters have gathered near my grandfather: a young woman, dressed heavily, tending to a child. An old man just down the bench, outfitted in an expensive, tan overcoat; the old man keeps watching, with a hangdog look, a newstand where commuters are stopping, picking up the Prague paper, then moving on quickly.

My grandfather looks at the newpaper displayed there in the vendor's rack. There is a large picture of Reinhard Heydrich on the front page. How much, this day in December, does my grandfather know about the 'Reichsprotektor'? It was Heydrich's contrived attack on the Gleiwitz German radio transmitter in August, 1939 (using concentration camp bodies dressed in Polish uniforms) that had given Hitler his excuse to begin the war. It is Heydrich who, under the Nacht and Nebel

Erlass (Night and Fog Decree) conceived by Hitler, seizes Czech citizens identified as "endangering German security"—kidnaps them and spirits them to Germany, where they are murdered and buried, their families left with no trace of what has happened. Thousands have disappeared this way. In a little over a month, at the Wannsee conference in Berlin, Heydrich, as the architect of the "Final Solution," will lay out his proposal to erase eleven million Jews from the earth.

The Reichsprotektor lives just outside Prague in a villa that once belonged to a Jewish sugar magnate. In newspaper photographs Heydrich sports perfect Aryan children and a blonde wife: Frau Heydrich has added bathrooms and a swimming pool to their new residence using concentration camp labor. At night, the Reichsprotektor tends to extramarital interests: he has a voracious sexual appetite, and an obsession with humiliating prostitutes.

He dreams of becoming the Nazi ruler of the Slavs from Bohemia cast into Russia. And he has his eye on a greater star as well: to one day replace his Fuehrer as the leader of the Reich. He is a most likely candidate.

My grandfather stares at the face in the newspaper, at the crooked nose and the strange, vacant cruelty of the eyes. I sense that he is appalled by those eyes.

Another announcement now: another train arriving. A door opens at the far end of the hall and German nurses in uniform come from it: they wear white caps with crosses and blue overcoats, and they are followed by Czech commuters who separate from them in the hall. Many Wehrmacht soldiers follow: coming from the door, speaking rapidly, their boots and voices echo loudly through the station. The flood of them breaks as it reaches the benches, but the soldiers hardly look at my grandfather and the other commuters sitting there. My grandfather overhears two of the young men having a discussion about a BMW motorcycle one of them wishes to buy—an engine of three-hundred and fifty cubic centimeters, a *feine machine*! Another pair talks about a girl in Munich. The Czechs, my grandfather with them, look away from the soldiers, but old Josef looks up at them after they are by, at their straight, proud bearing, and in this moment he is ashamed that he ever fought on the side of any German.

God what a thing! my grandfather thinks, staring at the floor. His son in a coal mine. Mira, who he saw today in the afternoon, working in a funeral home—young beautiful Mira walking in these streets with SS men who dress in black, who hate humanity. It breaks old Josef's heart.

He looks at his Doxa—6:20, and now comes the announcement: *Vlak do Plzně připraven k odjezdn v 18:20 hodin na kolejí číslo 12.* The train for Plsen is ready on track 12. My grandfather walks out to the dock where more commuters have gathered, waiting, the train slowly making its way toward them. He feels dizzy after the standing and walking, and there is numbness in his fingers. His right leg throbs.

His breath rises into the winter air, and a cloudy night is arriving with no stars. He will be glad when his train pulls into snow-covered Radnice; his Barbora will be waiting for him, and they will walk down into the village together to home, to dinner and bed.

That same night, as my grandfather slept with his restless dreams, two Czech parachutists—Resistance fighters who had been sent from England—drifted onto snowy fields just east of Plsen. They quickly gathered their chutes, and scuttled into hiding. Their names were Jan Kubiš and Josef Gabčik, both sergeants in the Czech army, and they had trained for months in Scotland for this chance to strike at the Nazis. Their mission, designed by Winston Churchill and Edvard Beneš, was called *Anthropoid*: the assassination of Reinhard Heydrich.

History next finds them five months later, on 27 May, 1942, at a bend in a street in Holesovice, near Prague, where the Reichprotektor drove each morning en route to the city. There the Resistance men waited for Heydrich's limousine to approach. Gabčik stepped in front of the dark green Mercedes as it made the turn, its black SS flag rippling. He dropped his raincoat, raised a Sten sub-machine gun, and pulled the trigger. The gun jammed. Kubiš, prepared for the possibility, threw a bomb at the car from the opposite side of the street. It exploded against the rear wheel. Heydrich was mortally wounded, with a broken rib, a ruptured diaphragm, and fragments from the explosion in his spleen. He died seven days later.

As Churchill and Beneš had hoped, fear spread quickly through the Nazi ranks that the Heydrich killing would be followed by more assassination attempts, perhaps even one on the Fuehrer himself. A reward of ten million Czech crowns (one million German marks) was offered for the arrest of the parachutists, and the sum was doubled a few days later. It was announced, constantly, on the radio and posted on billboards and in newspapers. Crisp, terrifying rules accompanied this enticement: anyone who disobeyed the Czech curfew of nine p.m. was shot without question. All Czechs over fifteen were required to register with the police: if they did not do so they and anyone harboring them would be shot. Anyone who hid the assassins would be shot, along with his or her entire families. Many family executions, according to American Intelligence sources of the time, were already taking place, sometimes at random: "...the Germans do not seem to have ... any clearer intention," one American intelligence report said, "than the satisfaction of their rage."

The Nazis swept through Radnice. A group of Wehrmacht soldiers came to my grandparents' home, where my grandfather was upstairs in bed, his heart failing. My grandmother, relieved that the soldiers were not SS, asked the Germans not to disturb her husband. They said they would not. They sat downstairs with my grandmother and father. One of them noticed a mandolin on the wall.

"We are supposed to spend one-half hour here," he told my grandmother. "Do you mind if we play some music to pass the time?"

My grandmother told them she did not mind. In that strange, horrifying day, the mandolin played by the Nazis sang through the rooms of the Hůrka home.

On the ninth of June, in the early morning, the Nazis came to the small town of Lidice, near the coal mines of Kladno. They had erroneous information that the villagers had at some point conspired with the parachutists. All one-hundred and ninety-five women and ninety-five children in town were seized and taken away. Most would be brought to the Ravensbrueck and Gneisenau concentration camps in Germany, never to be seen again. Some of the women under the age of twenty-five were destined to serve in German brothels;

four pregnant Lidice women, close to giving birth, would be sent to a hospital in Prague, where their newborns would be murdered. The mothers would then be brought to Ravensbrueck as well.

On Czechoslovak radio, an announcer's voice shook as he reported the last known facts of Lidice: one hundred seventy-two males over the age of fifteen were herded into one area and shot in groups of ten. A detail of Czech Jews from Terezín buried their corpses in a mass grave. Nineteen other Lidice men, who during the initial killing were working in the Kladno mines, were hunted down and killed. The homes and buildings of Lidice were set on fire and bulldozed to the ground.

Hitler threatened that the fate of Lidice would be the fate of all Czechs, if the assassins were not discovered.

Kubiš and Gabčik had hidden in the crypt of the Church of St. Cyril and St. Methodius in Prague along with five other parachutists who had helped them. Their plan, hatched in collusion with the priests of the church, was to remain in hiding for a brief time and then, locked in coffins, to be spirited away slowly in a funeral procession. If it had not been for a parachutist on the outside turned traitor, they might have made it.

But when Hitler ordered more reprisals—this time the murder of thirty-thousand politically active Czechs, Sergeant Karel Curda, a parachutist who had been hiding outside of the city, walked into the Prague Gestapo headquarters and set the Nazis on a swift path to the church.

The Nazis stormed the church at 4:10 on the morning of June 18. There a siege—four hundred SS troops against seven parachutists—went on for seven hours. Finally, with their last bullets, the parachutists shot themselves.

But the Nazi retributions for the killing of Heydrich continued. A few days after the battle at the church, the village of Ležáky, where a Resistance transmitter had been discovered, suffered the same fate as Lidice. All of the adults, including women, were massacred and of the children only two, considered worthy of Germanization, are known to have survived. Later that summer, two hundred and fifty-two relatives and friends who had aided the parachutists were brought to Prague, interrogated, tortured, and shown the heads of the seven parachutists impaled on spikes. Reports by the Gestapo expressed bafflement at the patriotism of these prisoners. The chief of the Prague Gestapo wrote on 25 June that they ". . . took a pronounced Czech, chauvinist, anti-German stance, especially the women . . . They were often heard to say: 'We are proud to die for our country.'"

In September, the priests of the Church of St. Cyril and St. Methodius were executed before a firing squad. A month later, at the Mauthausen concentration camp in Germany, the relatives and friends of the parachutists were murdered: the men were shot and the women and children died in the gas chambers.

When I think of this time I often think of how that mandolin was, that day in June, somehow an angel of mercy for my family. I think of my grandfather alone in bed, hearing the sounds of the Wehrmacht on Švehlova street, and the pounding at the front door. Then the mandolin music: making him wonder, giving him brief peace; for the moment, his family was all right. I imagine a German soldier, singing and laughing with his comrades in the living room below, striking the strings with the pick, and the golden color of the instrument against his field gray.

The mandolin now sits in my parents' home in Vermont, and has not been played for years. But when I was a boy my father played an old Bohemian tune on it for me, again and again, as often as I requested.

Barbora Kublová as a teenager.

CHAPTER THREE

THE MARTYRS, THE CATHEDRAL, AND AN EVENING AT 139 VINOHRADSKÁ

Mira had set me up with a city tour, saying that it would be best if I got an overall view of Prague, and then chose what I would like to see more closely. It sounded like a fair idea to me.

En route to the Čedok bus tour building in downtown Prague we went through crowded Wenceslas Square. It is an avenue, really, headed on its upper end by the National Museum. Near the museum, below the great statue of St. Wenceslas astride his horse, we stopped at a homemade monument that has stayed there, in a small circle, since the revolution of 1989. The monument, a kind of circle of martyrs, is made up of a Czech flag, pictures, epitaphs and names on placards set into the ground on wooden stakes—tributes to heroes of the republic and victims of Communist tyranny. Everywhere, there are fresh flowers and wreaths, and this day the sun was out and wind dashed through ribbons and flowers below us and Mira and I looked for a long while at the pictures.

Here was Tomáš Masaryk, and his son Jan, who was murdered by the Communists during the coup of 1948. And here was the picture, also, of Jan Palach, the Charles University student who burned himself to death on this spot in 1969, as a protest against the Russian invasion which ended the "Prague Spring." I remembered this time. I was seven when First Secretary of the Communist Party Alexander Dubček led Czechoslovakia toward "socialism with a human face" or what the Soviet Union finally (and correctly) interpreted as freedom. Photographs from *Life* magazine came back to me as I had seen them then; first the moments of brief freedom in that summer of 1968: of a pretty young model, leaning against an ancient wall; of Prague beneath a midsummer moon; of Brezhnev and Dubček clasping hands in a show of unity, even while the Soviets conspired to crush Dubček's leadership. And then the violence of August, 1968: Soviet tanks rumbling madly through this Square, stoned and smeared with paint by defiant crowds; an old woman crying, holding up a picture of the Czech leaders she believed in, and Soviet soldiers, brandishing their weapons at Czechs in the streets. The Soviets had quickly reimprisoned the country. That late summer remains for me my first awareness of the brutality of totalitarianism, and I remembered now my father pacing before our old Zenith black and white television like a caged animal, watching the pictures of the Soviet tanks, of his old home being invaded once again, of the last pictures of Dubček that would be seen until 1989.

Above us, St. Wenceslas boldly looked over his square. This "good king," in actuality a prince of the Premyslid Dynasty, had always been, in legend, a spiritual tonic for the Czech people. His statue here was frequently a gathering place for patriotic demonstrations during Communist years. In August of 1968, a national flag was placed in his hand in defiance of the Soviets; below the statue, at the start of the invasion, a fourteen year-old boy waving his own Czech tricolor was killed by Russian soldiers. At the end of the crisis a black flag of mourning replaced the Czech flag in St. Wenceslas' hand, with a message beneath: "We Don't Give Up." Five months later, on January 16, 1969, Jan Palach drenched himself with gasoline here, and lit himself afire.

Palach's face stared out from his placard with a kind of vulnerable hope, eighteen years old. I thought of my own students this age, and of the insanity of a human in flames, and of a system that had turned humanity inside out. I thought of my father, locked in prisons I had yet to see, and there was a tugging at my throat and eyes that I had difficulty controlling for a moment. I thought: there is a lesson in these brave faces and names below me to last for centuries.

The Čedok bus was clean and modern and air-conditioned and built for tourists. And I was exhausted, somehow, physically and emotionally, from the overseas trip and the few things I had seen and learned, so that it was nice to sink back in the bus seat and wave so long for the afternoon to Mira and just be on my own for a while in the air-conditioned smoothness while the driver worried and negotiated his way through the crowds and narrow streets. Tourists packed the stone sidewalks of Na přikopě street in their colorful regalia, many of them students from Germany, France, and the other countries of Europe, and sometimes the crowds were so deep that you could not see the lower faces of the buildings, and you couldn't see up very well either, because as you move through Prague many of the streets are so narrow and the ancient buildings so tall that much of what our woman guide pointed out in an unsteady English and French mixture went unheeded by me. I gave up after a while, and only looked up when the guide called out the name of Pankrác prison. The building was in the distance, large and gray, and the guide was saying that President Havel had been held there—and then we were quickly by it and I wished I'd had more time to look at it. My father had been imprisoned there also.

Soon we were on the winding road called Chotkova, up toward Hradčany Castle, the bus swinging and twisting through the turns, and there was Prague on a sunlit day below us, a beautiful city of six hundred spires. There was a slight haze above the metropolis on this springtime day, and I thought of all the people within this place, selling, buying, shouting, telling, flirting, cheating, making love, giving birth—and all of that happening through a thousand years. It seemed remarkable that the city still stood now, vibrating with the continuum of human sounds, the constant music of human yearning.

The bus stopped and we walked on to Loreta Square, a place of cobblestones and green, sand and rust-burnished buildings, and everywhere the same hip-shingled roofs. The Square is dominated by the white and black Loreto monastery with its distinctive baroque bell tower on one side, and on the other by the massive Černín palace, five hundred feet long with

Corinthian half-columns running across its upper storey. Our troop stopped before the monastery, one band of tourists among many. A number of us pulled out cameras for pictures. I took out my old Pentax, to remember the general fix and breadth of Černín palace for my writing, but I found quickly, looking through the camera lens, that you could not get all of it—the magnificence of the white building beneath the sun— into the rectangular box the camera gave you to peer through. The ancient monastery rose to my right above the crowd. Built in 1626, it stood pristine, its towers sharp against the blue of sky. I snapped a few pictures of it, and then followed as we moved on to the castle.

At the castle gates were the Czech guards, dressed in their new, blue, white and red uniforms that had been fashioned by the costume designer of the movie *Amadeus*, at the request of President Havel. The guards stood stoically, a step outside the small, striped shelters built for them in case of rain. Their white-gloved hands rested on rifles. Tourists stood beside them to have pictures taken. Above, on either side of the ornate entrance to the castle, huge sculptures of giants brandished knives and clubs, locked in battle there since their creation in the eighteenth century. I walked with a kindly, middle aged couple, Keith and Dorothy Hanney of Australia, who had recently been to France, and they told me a little about their trip as we went through a crowded courtyard with buildings erected by Maria Theresa. There were so many people here that funneling through the gateways into the next, large courtyard was a tight affair, and then we were into the main complex, or Third Courtyard, of government buildings, facing an entrance to the magnificent St. Vitus cathedral. Here, our guide explained, pointing to the governmental area, was the place where President Havel went each morning to his offices, and I wondered how he got through the crowds—in a limo?

I thought about what a glorious view the president must have had from his work space, of the face of the cathedral. Parts of St. Vitus date back to 925, and much of it is still in the original Gothic construction of the fourteenth and fifteenth centuries. The great church towered over us and I tried to take a picture of it, but once again there was no way to get my subject completely into the camera frame. Others tried as well: at one point, I saw a young teen-aged girl lying on the ground with a camera, looking through it up, up. I doubt that she was successful.

The cathedral has a kind of ancient, deep burnt-orange color that tells you it has been around a lot longer than you have. I leaned way back with Keith and Dorothy, and watched it rise into the sky.

Then we were being quite surely pushed with the crowd in the direction of one of the cathedral entrances, and as we were bumped and jostled Keith leaned to me and said, "Keep ahold of your wallet." In Paris, I'd found out earlier, he'd been relieved of his on a subway. I had just about enough time to think about the strangeness of worrying about theft on the way into a church, and then we were inside.

There is a kind of golden light within this, the largest ecclesiastical building in Prague, and I had to stop to take in the volume of the place. Light comes in through Bohemian glass windows, and the ceiling arches toward the heavens. Fourteen saints, towering above you, adorn the pillars of the inner structure, and the cathedral has twenty-one chapels, each a work of art.

In one of the chapel windows a dazzling array of vivid blues and bright oranges glowed at us, designs of kings and queens and monks in cloaks with their hands raised, two fingers together in a sign of truth. There were trees in vivid green: mothers and daughters looked out beyond us as if at some mystery only they might understand: pilgrims beneath their hoods looked to the heavens at night. And above all of it, in glowing blue and brown, Christ opened his arms above this world. When the light strikes the glass correctly, as it did this afternoon, the effect is extraordinary.

We were approaching St. Wenceslas Chapel, a room with a golden steeple that once held the wafers and wine for the Holy Communion of royalty. A large crowd at the right was shuffling forward toward the door, and I pushed in with Keith and Dorothy to try and get a glimpse. But, as polite as all of the tourists were in trying to respect one another's space, the three of us finally grew discouraged—I was close enough to see the ceilings of gold, a room so ornate as to dazzle the eyes, and then I turned away, determined to read about it, and let the pictures come to my head that way. I went again with the Hanneys to the center of the cathedral, and we all together looked up as if at heaven. "You know, we've just finished a tour at Notre Dame," Keith said, "and it doesn't even compare to this."

Here as a boy, my father came with Mira and my grandfather to see the tombs of the ancient Czech kings in the crypt below us, closed this day. Here, for the first time, my father once told me, the history he'd read and heard about became real to him—those kings whose stories he'd followed were there, before him, and had truly been alive once. Mira had told me of those trips to Prague, too, and standing here in the cathedral I imagined one such journey: my grandfather on the train to the city with his children, dressed formally as always, leaning forward to peer through a window. Mira had told me he liked to point out the castle Karlštejn, near Beroun, which you could see across the fields from the train. *Look there, Mira. Look there, Josef,* he would say. *There on that hill lived King Charles the Fourth. He was to all those people hundreds of years ago what President Masaryk is now, the leader of our nation.* I imagined my father and Mira looking from the train across a bright spring field at the king's castle beyond.

My grandmother didn't like to travel as much as her husband, so usually the children took these trips to the city with their father only. He would take them to the gardens of Pĕtrín Hill, and to the "Mirror Maze" there from the Exhibition of 1891 where they could howl with laughter at their strange reflections. They walked together to the president's entrance of the castle where once a guard leaned down to Mira and told her that maybe, when she got a little older, she might be invited to one of the president's dances.

While in the city, they stayed with Uncle Leo in his flat just beneath Hradčany at 21 Nerudova Street. The children drove around Prague with their uncle in the snazzy American Dodge that he kept parked just down the hill, in front of the Romanian Embassy. At night, they could look up from their bedroom and see the president's flag flying over the castle.

Our tour group walked out of the cathedral now, through the courtyard and to the wall that overlooks that area where Leo once lived, called the "Little Quarter" of Prague. The city from here seemed to be a blanket of the red roofs and spires, and there, looking very close on this warm day, was massive St. Nicholas cathedral, a shape I recognized from a painting in my home when I was a boy. I turned back and looked up at the president's flag, thinking as I did so how odd it was that that flag of truth had, since the Communist coup of 1948, flown over crooked governments. Until three years ago a Communist government had ruled with an iron fist here, living under the strange delusion that if it could simply *contain* human emotion, and *funnel* human ambition, sooner or later everyone would comply with its philosophy. For a time in my own country, it was fashionable to make fun of those who suggested that the ambition of Soviet Russia was world dominance. I remember, in the early nineteen-eighties, many arguments with fellow college students about this. Some years later, at the University of Iowa, I did not challenge a student Communist group advertising the sickle and hammer in the campus center. I had learned by then that you could not explain about a system divorced from the human heart, that one had to experience it, in some way, personally, for it to become real. But it seemed foolish for anyone to suggest that the Communists did *not* wish to dominate the world. Of course they did: that was their ultimate security, and they were ruthless in seeing it done.

Now, in 1993, the Soviet Empire had collapsed, and perhaps with it the impetus that kept the Communist animal hungry for new blood. The Communist governments that still existed would increasingly feed off themselves and would disintegrate from within; still, I grieved for the human beings that had suffered and would continue to under the system. I thought about the brave student dissidents in China, murdered after their demonstration in Tiananmen Square, and how the Chinese government had forced their parents to buy the bullets used in the executions. Images of these violations blended before me with the astonished, anguished faces in St. Wenceslas Square in August, 1968, and with the frequent moments in history when dictators, unable to coerce or lie their way to dominance, brought out their guns.

In the evenings, because of my broken leg, I was confined to sitting in the same chair I folded out to sleep on, my leg up on pillows on another chair, and as Mira put together dinner I would read the history of the places I'd seen that day or prepare for the following day or write letters and postcards home. I asked, on the first few occasions, whether I could help Mira with the dinner preparations, but always I was refused, which in the end seemed quite practical since the kitchen was small and I would only have furthered Mira's exasperation.

So there I sat with my leg up, reading about King Charles the Fourth, and about Jan Hus, and the Hussite military genius, Žižka. I read about the Czech Resistance in World War II and the fight at the Church of St. Cyril and St. Methodius. I told Mira I wanted to go to the church and she said from the kitchen, "It's not far from here, we will go."

In one small traveler's guide I found reference to the legend of the ghost soldiers of St. Wenceslas; this ancient legion of the good king, immortalized in Smetana's *Má Vlast* (My Fatherland), slept beneath Blaník mountain in the south of the country, and would rise from the fields of Bohemia to take up the sword when the nation was in danger. I mentioned it to Mira, and she said that she'd wondered often where the ghost soldiers were all these years. I said quietly that I guessed they'd finally come.

Some nights after dinner we watched television on Mira's old black and white Tessla. The programs were punctuated with many commercials: high energy advertisements for diapers, cat food, chewing gum, dishwashing liquid, deodorant soap and perfume. Before the news, I always looked forward to a five-minute aerobic workout sponsored by *Playboy* magazine, complete with stunning models gyrating enthusiastically. America was represented through an oft-running cigarette ad of a cowboy squinting his eyes, á la Clint Eastwood, as he took a drag. I could follow the news pretty well, although sometimes it was frustrating, trying to make out President Clinton's face and words behind the Czech graphics and the fast voice of an interpreter. The war was raging in Bosnia and Clinton and Europe and the United Nations were trying to figure out what to do about it: the Serbs had already conquered seventy percent of Bosnia's territory, and internment camps were being compared to the concentration camps of fifty years before. There were also follow-up stories about the recent battle between the Branch Davidians and US agents in Waco, Texas, and footage of the compound burning. Locally, the Slovaks wanted compensation for the Czech use of the original Czechoslovakian tricolor flag. I could tell, when they interviewed Czech Prime Minister Klaus about it, that his response was something to the effect of: *they* were the ones who wanted to split from *us*.

One evening we settled in to watch *The Birthday Party*, a Czech film about a woman in the nineteen-fifties whose birthday party is suddenly raided by the

StB. The secret police have come to arrest her. Before leaving, she tells her stunned guests that she will continue the party with them in a few years time. And then she is taken away.

Most of the story takes place after the twenty years of her detention, when she has returned to her old home, a mansion confiscated by the State and now lived in by a group of apathetic, frightened tenants. Of those she has once known and trusted, only her former butler seems to have the courage to spend time with her. She searches in vain for work, for new lodging, in a kind of determined but hopeless existence. Finally she and the butler decide together, alone, to pick up the birthday party where they left off, in the now decrepit parlor of the old residence. When the butler brings a tray out to his friend with tea and crackers and a rose, he realizes she has died.

"That is just what it was like," Mira said, emotional, after I had switched off the television. "You cannot imagine. Just what it was like."

Then, well into the night, I heard those true stories from Mira: of the StB parked, some nights, across Vinohradská Street. They would come to the apartment and say, threatening, to my grandmother and Mira, You see, we have Josef in the car, and Mira and Barbora would look out the window and sure enough, someone in the car would be dressed in a jacket and hat similar to those my father had worn. And the StB men would say, It would be better for all of us if you would tell us what you know about his activities.

For sentimental reasons, my grandmother kept a coat of my father's hanging in the apartment. Sometimes the StB burst into the flat at night and felt the coat to see if it was warm. They forced my grandmother at gunpoint before them into the kitchen, convinced my father was in there with a gun. They came again and again. They brought Mira to the government buildings at Hradčany for long nights of questioning. Of course she could tell them nothing.

I heard of how my grandmother burned all the pictures she had of my father over the toilet, afraid to let them fall into Communist hands, afraid that this would help turn her boy over to them. And so she did out of love what the Communists were doing to my father out of hate: she erased him from history.

No Mira, I thought, you are correct. There is a part of me that cannot fathom how it was.

Grandfather Josef (third from left) with his Sokol group, just before leaving to fight with the Austro-Hungarian army, 1914.

CHAPTER FOUR

A RECKONING

In the ruins of Adolf Hitler's Reich, Joseph Stalin moved quickly to capture what was left of Czechoslovakia. Czechoslovak Communists had been jockeying for power within the country since the days of Tomáš Masaryk, and in the chaos of the war's end they were organized and powerful. From the outside, Stalin had been adamant in his discussions with the West that his troops should liberate Prague and most of the country. Though Winston Churchill raised strong and repeated objections to this, the Red Army rolled into the Bohemian capital in May of 1945, as George Patton (who had beaten them there) waited furiously and helplessly outside of the city, ordered to halt.

The Czechs were a people exhausted with conflict. German plunder and destruction had run up a bill of some fourteen billion dollars in the nation: two hundred thousand Czechs had perished in the concentration camps. An additional thirty-eight thousand Czechs who had worked in the Underground had been executed by the Gestapo. After six years of Nazism, war and upheaval, many in the country were weary and willing to accept that, in Czechoslovakia at least, communism and capitalism might exist benevolently, side by side.

They could not, of course. Vladimír Ilyich Ulyanov Lenin had once written: "As long as capitalism and socialism exist, we cannot live in peace; in the end one or the other will triumph—its funeral dirge will be sung over the Soviet republic or over world capitalism." He encouraged his followers not to be hindered by morality in the fight to establish authoritarian rule. "We have to use any ruse, dodge, trick, cunning, unlawful methods, concealment, veiling the truth . . ." he said. "Communist morality is the morality which serves this struggle."

Joseph Stalin put a careful plan into place. His Communist regime-in-waiting, headed by the Czech Communist Klement Gottwald, would work within the parliamentary system of a liberated Czechoslovakia to win elections. It seemed the most surefooted way to win over a people who had fresh memories of a vibrant democracy. If that did not work, there were other ways, tried and tested, to seize control.

While making a game face of working hand in hand with the reestablished President Beneš, Communist politicians reminded their constituents that it was only their Russian Slav brothers who had offered help during the dark days of the Munich crisis (neglecting to mention Stalin's later agreements with Hitler). The Communist Party pushed for the extradition of Germans from Bohemia, a popular position with the Czech population. And though Tomáš Masaryk had once been condemned by the Party as a "puppet" of western imperialists, he now emerged in official Communist statements as a "working-class hero." Slowly, under the guise of recreating a democratic republic, the Party infiltrated and solidified its grip on the country.

The Ministry of Information, under Communist control, kept a tight rein on radio and the press and even on materials used by the press. The Party diligently constructed accusations of fascist sympathy and collusion against all who opposed them, and they worked to gain control of the police.

In the first parliamentary elections of 1946, the Communist Party drew thirty-eight percent of the popular vote—a majority that earned them nearly half the seats in parliament. When another party, the Social Democrats, chose to unite with them, suddenly the Communist Party had fifty-one percent representation—and Edvard Beneš was forced to name Gottwald Premier of Czechoslovakia.

But Communist control of the economy did not deliver the new, worker's paradise that the Party had promised, and by 1947 the initial rush by the populace to embrace their Communist liberators was nearly still. That year, Beneš' National Socialist Party picked up five times as many memberships as did the Communists.

Gottwald, in concert with Stalin, put contingency plans into action. In the Slovak part of the country, where Communists controlled much of the security forces, a number of democratic ministers were suddenly arrested on the charge of "high treason." And through out Czechoslovakia, the Communist Interior Ministry began shadowing other important leaders, including Foreign Minister Jan Masaryk, closely. "Revolutionary Action Committees," political pressure groups, worked to insure that factories, farms and villages fell under Communist control. In early February, 1948, the Communists moved to take complete charge of the police in Prague. In protest, twelve non-Communist ministers in Beneš' cabinet resigned, giving the Communist Party a legal opening to take control of the country.

The Communists demanded that Beneš name a fully Communist cabinet. Beneš, a recent victim of two brain hemorrhages and only months away from death, resisted this final Communist pressure. The Party prepared for a violent overthrow of the country if he did not give in. The Army—solidly in Communist hands—was put on alert, and "People's Militia's," rogue groups similar to those that had worked early on for Hitler, were told to prepare for battle. The borders of Czechoslovakia were sealed and, over the next few months, as thousands would try to flee, the frontiers would tighten with heavy reinforcements. From the sidelines, the Soviet Union made veiled threats that Soviet military intervention was imminent.

Under protest, Beneš signed in the Communist cabinet on February 25, 1948. Quickly, those government officials sympathetic to democracy were thrown, often physically, out of their offices or imprisoned. Others fled the country. Democratic buildings were ransacked, essential documents stolen. Still Beneš fought on, with Masaryk by his side, both aware that the end was near, making a stand, perhaps, for history.

Jan Masaryk was the favorite son of his nation: Czechoslovakia had not forgotten how he had offered hope and determination from Britain during the Nazi occupation. At age sixty-one he was a last symbol of his father's bright democracy. As the Communists now swallowed his country, he remained defiant, carrying on with an attitude he had expressed a few months earlier, at a speech to war veterans on Žofín Island in Prague. Acknowledging that many of his countrymen were being condemned as "bourgeois reactionaries," Masaryk told them, "I proudly declare that I am one of the reactionaries and bourgeois . . . The word 'reaction' derives from the Latin word *'reagere.'* If your opinion is different and you act against something—you react. As long as I live and my mind works, I shall react, and if I do not agree with others, I shall say so. That is why I am one of the reactionaries . . . and I shall always react against evil in an orderly manner. 'Bourgeois' is the French word for citizen: I am proud to be a citizen of the Czechoslovak Republic, and I claim and accept all my civic rights and duties."

On the morning of March 9, 1948, Masaryk's body was found in the courtyard thirty feet below his apartment window at Černín palace. His eyes were wide open, and his fingernails were jammed full of paint and plaster. The bones of his legs were fractured so badly that they jutted out of the flesh at his heels. Bone fragments from his shattered feet were spread around him. There were signs of a ferocious struggle in the apartment overhead.

Rude Pravo, the official Communist newspaper, reported that he had committed suicide.

My father's troubles with the Communists started, strangely enough, with a romance. The year was 1945, and Josef was dating a young, pretty girl from Karlovy Vary, a famous spa one hundred kilometers west of Prague. He was stationed with a military unit there, and waiting to know if he would be accepted into the military academy of Hranice to train to be an officer—

his only chance for Air Force duty, since with a need for glasses he could not enter the Air Force directly as an enlisted man. Apparently my father did not express undying love to young Anna Kadečková, but someone else did, and Anna made her choice and was married. My father was accepted to military school and moved on with his studies and training.

But Anna would come back to haunt him.

In the meantime, Josef Hůrka earned a degree in Ballistics and Military Sciences and was commissioned as a lieutenant in the Czech Armed Forces. He took on an extensive background in commando tactics and fighting, a discipline that would help him one day more than he knew. After a short duty in Slovakia, he was stationed at the Air Force academy at Hradec Králové, some ninety-five kilometers east of Prague. In an atmosphere where much of the military faced execution if they defied Communist authorities, the Air Force, because it required highly-trained personnel, was the last service which had an abundance of anti-Communist officers. My father was one of these.

He befriended and admired those pilots who, during World War II, had flown with the British during the Battle of Britain. Because these men had close ties with the West, they were all suspect in the new atmosphere of Stalinist Czechoslovakia. And yet, for the time being, their services were indispensable. They believed that Communism was a passing and vulgar phase in their country, and that, in two or three years time, through revolt or reform, the Czech government would again be democratic. It was these men, and not the "reds," as they called them, that Josef sat with in the mess hall. Together, they did not spare the Communists in their jokes and discussions. And Communist ears were listening.

Josef had another, specific distinction: he had become a top ski racer in his country, and was asked by Communist authorities to preach the Party line to admiring youngsters. This he flatly refused.

By 1949, at the age of twenty-three, he was the deputy commander in an Air Force school for noncommissioned officers. Many of these officers became friends of his, and often they all went skiing together in an area called Krkonoše, a stunning mountain range on the northern border of Bohemia. They stayed in a mountain chalet which was so isolated that, a few days before they were to arrive, they flew a Buecker 104 biplane over the area and dropped a note tied to a rock at the front door of the lodge, so that the lodgekeeper would know how many rooms were needed for the weekend.

It was at about this time that Anna Kadečková sent Josef a letter. It was addressed to "MP" Hurka—a nickname Josef had earned one night, just after the end of the war, when he and some other Czech soldiers had stopped two American GIs from raping a Czech girl in Karlovy Vary, and had handed the men over to American military police. Anna said that she had gotten a divorce and, would Josef be interested in rekindling the relationship?

Josef took the train from Hradec Králové to Prague, and another from Prague to Karlovy Vary. It was a long journey, and he made it out of uniform—he had sprained his ankle the day before during exercises and, walking with a cane, had decided to dispose of the uniform and go more comfortably in civilian clothes.

Then he was back in the old spa town that he had not visited in four years, and when the door opened to his former girlfriend's apartment it was clear that Anna was prettier than ever. But there was another man in the apartment. He was about fifty, said he was an American, and had come to ask Anna to marry him and travel with him to Bombay. "I will make sure I take all of my money with me," he kept telling Anna. Josef inferred from this that the man was Jewish, an expatriate living in Prague perhaps, who was nervous about the Communist ring closing around him. Not long after Josef's arrival the man left, and a few confusing hours followed, with Anna trying to explain this unexpected situation and considering the Bombay marriage at the same time. She wasn't sure what to do. Finally, Josef left also, feeling saddened and a little used and angry, and altogether glad to be through with the whole fiasco.

At the academy, Communism was rooting itself in every aspect of Air Force life. Those higher-ranking officers who had close ties to the West were, one by one, being removed from the service and subjected to making a living for their families doing menial jobs. Four that Josef knew well escaped, flying a twin-engine bomber to a civilian airport in eastern Bohemia to pick up their wives and children and then going on to England.

The Communists approached Josef a number of times more in his capacity as an athlete to promote the Party line to children, and time and again he refused, growing more angry at this insistence, and feeling abandoned now that many of his friends were gone. He knew a number of athletes who had capitulated to Party pressure, just to get along, but it did not feel right, and he was angry at the arrogance of the Party and the way his friends had been treated. And in matters of principle he had always been stubborn.

On a Friday afternoon in late February, 1949, he was training alone in Krkonoše, shooting ski gates. When evening fell, he let his skis glide and, in a loose tuck formation, shushed down the mountain into the valley. As he neared the lodge, he saw two men standing by the entrance wearing heavy leather knee-length coats, a trademark of the secret police.

The men greeted him politely as he was taking off his skis.

"Are you Josef Hůrka?" one of them, the taller of the two, asked.

Josef glanced up. The men were standing with their hands in their coat pockets: he knew in those pockets were guns.

"Yes, I am Josef Hůrka."

The tall man pulled out StB identification and said they had orders to arrest him.

"What for?" Josef said.

"We have no idea," the man said. "We simply got a call to find you, and we're just following orders."

The men took Josef into the lodge, where the lodgekeeper and his wife stared at him, frightened, from the kitchen. He collected his things, and as the three men began the two-mile trek downhill to the road with dusk falling around them, they conversed easily.

"Why would we be sent to arrest you?" the taller StB agent asked. "What did you do?"

"I was just wondering the same thing myself," Josef said.

"Did you have plans to escape to the West?" the other agent asked.

"If I had," Josef said, "why would I ski on the northern border? Why not go to the border of West Germany?"

"Perhaps somebody made a mistake," the tall man said.

Night had fallen by the time the three of them made it to a local prison: it was a one-room cell, with about twenty inmates filling it already, sleeping in various positions on the dirt floor. An open metal bucket to the side served as a toilet. There was a horrible stench to the place, and Josef could not sleep. He sat to one side of the cell, his back against the bars, staring at the others and the night and thinking about his situation.

In the morning, the same StB men picked him up and brought him back to the academy at Hradec Králové. As the car went through the main gate of the academy, the sergeant in charge of the guard recognized Josef's face, and the guards lined up and presented arms. The two StB men laughed at this.

Josef was escorted to the office of Colonel Pristach, the academy head of the counter-espionage department. There, he was told that he had been picked up to prevent his escape from the country. He repeated what he had said to the StB: that it was absurd that he should try to escape to the north. But Pristach cut his arguments off, and Josef was brought to the academy prison, where he stayed an afternoon and night. Most of the guards knew Josef and tried to make his stay as easy as possible. Some told him they would try to let his family know what had happened to him. Others, Communists, were delighted at his turn of fate, and made no secret of it.

In the morning, he could see through the prison

window many of his friends going to their offices or standing in line at the mess hall. It was a strange feeling, watching them from inside the bars of his cell.

Another pair of StB agents arrived soon and they drove him to a house near the edge of the city which looked deceptively like any medium-sized residential home. The outside walls were in a mild state of deterioration, with some of the masonry chipped. The entrance was normal, sedate, and would not have led anyone to believe that anything unusual happened in the quiet building.

But just inside the entrance there was another door made of thick steel bars and guarded by two large, muscled men in blue coveralls. Red armbands on their left sleeves signified that these men were members of the "Workers' Militia," the paramilitary organization run by the Communist-controlled Interior Ministry of Czechoslovakia. Josef was brought to an elevator that went down. Down, down, three floors, to a corridor with floor, walls and ceiling of reinforced concrete. A number of steel doors lined the left wall. One of these, about in the middle, was opened for Josef. The steel door was closed behind him and the bolt locked in place.

The cell was about nine feet long and six wide and it had a low ceiling, all also in concrete. A ragged mattress lay in the corner. Against one wall was a table and chair. There was a toilet bowl with running water. The heavy steel door had a small peep hole near the top for guards to look in, and a foot-square hatch in the middle for food delivery.

About four hours into Josef's stay, the door opened, and a man was shoved inside with such force that he landed, hard, against the far side of the cell. The steel door slammed shut behind him.

"Bastards," the man said. He had a hard, unshaven face, and dark eyes. He rubbed his arms and legs. "I had an argument with the guard and he kicked me," he said. "He has no right to do that."

Then the newcomer seemed to take in Josef, completely, for the first time. "I am glad to see that I shall not be alone," he said. "I am Franta Zeman." He held out his hand.

"Josef Hůrka," Josef said. "I'm sorry we have to meet under such conditions."

"This is my third week here," the man said. "But they haven't gotten a thing out of me—nothing at all." He looked at the door. "They can beat me as much as they want, but I'm not going to betray my friends."

For a long time, the two men sat close together, speaking in low tones. Josef mostly listened, convinced that the man had been through three harrowing weeks and needed a sympathetic ear. Zeman seemed to be fortifying himself as he talked about the need to remain faithful to the resistance group he belonged to, regardless of the cost.

Josef had heard of these resistance groups. Called *skupina* in Czech (meaning "group"), they were generally small bands of Czech patriots formed after the war to resist the Communist movement. Some were better organized than others: often, skupinas were funded by American Intelligence. Sometimes the precursor to the Russian KGB, called NKVD in 1949, in conjunction with the StB, started their own "skupinas" and, once they had drawn in a sufficient number of Czech patriots, rounded them up and put them in jail. Whether caught through this subterfuge or as part of genuine resistance groups, members of these skupinas now filled Czech prisons.

The two men talked into the night and finally fell asleep. When he woke some hours later, Josef was surprised to see his companion staring strangely and with reflection at him. The man's expression brightened, however, when he realized that Josef was awake.

"Good morning," Franta Zeman said. "I have a suggestion."

The two men had, since their initial introductions, in Czech custom, been addressing one another as "Mr. Hůrka" and "Mr. Zeman." "How about we do away with the formalities," Zeman said now, "and go by first names? I am Anton."

Anton! Josef did his best not to show his surprise. Instead, he thought quickly about their earlier conversation, and how this StB plant, whoever he was, had returned again and again to the subject of Karlovy Vary. It was suddenly clear to Josef that the Communists had been following him on his fateful romantic trip there—but to what end?

He had made the trip out of uniform, with a limp that might have appeared as a disguise. He had seen the American and had not reported the foreigner's presence to his superior officers.

And near that old spa town were the Jachymov uranium mines, one of the few places in the world where Uranium-238 was mined for the construction of the atomic bomb (another, in use by the Americans, was in South Africa. They had to pay for the material, while the Russians got it here free, using prison-camp labor). This was probably it, the reason for all this: the Communists thought he was somehow involved with a skupina himself and providing the Americans with intelligence about the mine. His old girlfriend's calling him "MP" on the letter couldn't have helped much, either.

"Anton's" conversation, sure enough, swung again to the subject of Karlovy Vary, and now Josef told the plant his story in detail, trying to portray himself as a bit of a klutz with women, and a sportsman disinterested in politics. Sometime later, when they'd gone over it a few times, "Anton" said he was having a change of heart. He was tired of being beaten, he said. It wasn't worth it anymore. He got up and banged on the door.

"I shall talk," he shouted. "I shall tell all. Take me to your officer." The guards came quickly and took him away. Josef hoped he had put his story solidly enough in the man's head, though he didn't have much faith in an operative who had forgotten his own alias.

Josef was alone again, but not unhappy about being rid of the mental chess he'd played for hours with the plant. He did thirty push-ups to revive his spirits. He flushed the toilet bowl and waited for it to fill with clean water. He took a long drink.

Soon after, the door opened and two of the Militia guards brought in boxes of die-cut paper with gluelines on it. They brusquely demonstrated how to fold and glue the individual pieces to make envelopes.

"Work work work," one of the guards shouted at him. "The more you work, the more food you get. Work will make your stomach feel good."

Josef took the materials without saying anything, and as the two men left he thought grimly of the sign at the entrance of Nazi concentration camps: *Albeit macht frei* (work sets you free).

The guards were the last people he saw for a long

time, perhaps even weeks. During what was apparently night, the lights were turned on at odd intervals to confuse his sleeping habits. Food was rare and usually consisted of thin soup with one vegetable in it or gruel and a scrap of bread.

He made himself exercise on a routine schedule. He recited poems and passages from his favorite books, and hummed songs he knew. He worked out math problems in his head. Sometimes he concentrated on one sentence, repeating it several hundred times: *You will not break down . . . you will not break down.*

The silence of the prison was disturbed only by the sounds of men being beaten and tortured in the cells nearby. Sometimes Josef could hear the angry voices of the StB raised at the arrogance, the utter uselessness, of resistance to them in this place. Josef would close his eyes, and try to give strength to his fellow prisoners.

The envelopes kept coming through the door. At some point, after a long, careful search of his cell, Josef found a small piece of pencil. The discovery thrilled him. From that moment on, on the inside of envelopes he was folding and gluing, he wrote patriotic Czech slogans and obscene words about Stalin and the Communist party. Sometimes, when he closed his eyes to sleep, he imagined that the envelopes got into the hands of young patriotic Czechs who, realizing a prisoner had made them, would be inspired to fight this cancer in his country. By God, if he ever made it out of here, he sure would.

But that was looking more and more doubtful. His body, assaulted by constant hunger, had deteriorated, despite his exercising. He felt horrible. He was unable to shave and now had long whiskers. He was still in the same ski pants, sneakers, socks, t-shirt and underwear, sports shirt and sweater that he'd been brought in. He washed his clothes in the toilet and tried to keep his body clean, but it was a depressing battle.

And then one day the door opened and two of the Militia guards stepped in briskly, followed by a middle-aged man wearing the long StB leather jacket. The Militia men made a thorough search of Josef's cell, and then were sent out by the StB man with a reminder to stay nearby.

The older man sat at the table and stared at Josef.

"They aren't taking very good care of you," he said, finally. "I came here to get truthful answers to several questions. You by now must understand what this place is and I am sure that you would like to get out of here. I may be the key to your release. On the other hand, if you don't cooperate, things may get a lot worse."

He opened his briefcase and took out a number of typewritten pages. He spread them across the desk. He pointed to his right. "You stand here," he said.

Josef realized, as he moved to where the man's finger was pointing, that it wasn't a bad vantage point. By shifting his weight, he could occasionally make out some of the information over the StB man's shoulder when the man glanced down at his notes. In this way Josef could prepare, a little bit, for what was coming up.

First the man wanted to know about Josef's boyhood and education. What was life like with Josef's bourgeois parents? What were his activities during the war years? Did he cooperate with the Nazis? Did he fully understand what was happening in his country now—that the workers had taken over and were leading everyone toward a rich and beautiful life in a class-less society?

The preaching continued for a long time and seemed designed, Josef thought, to get him angry. It succeeded, but he held his tongue. A few times it occurred to him, looking at the tight, angry face that turned up to him, that the StB man might simply be a fanatic. When more detailed questions started, Josef worked on creating the same simple picture of himself that he had for the StB plant, of a young, upstanding lieutenant skilled in sports and technical matters, but fairly naive when it came to politics.

Soon enough, the questions targeted Karlovy Vary. When the man turned to look at his notes, Josef caught a glimpse of . . . *but went to Karlovy Vary, out of uniform, leaning on a cane, perhaps to alter his appearance.*

"Who was the American you met?" Josef was asked.

"He was there only briefly," Josef said. "And I wasn't meeting with him. He was there courting the girl."

Josef explained the situation: yes, he said, he knew it was a standing regulation to report encounters with foreign nationals but he'd spoken only a greeting to the man. He knew he'd been wrong there.

No, he hadn't passed any state secrets to the American: and no, he hadn't told him anything about the aircraft used at the academy or the pilot training or the number of officers and cadets present. Frankly, these were hardly secrets: the Air Force planes were simply old German Arados and a few ME109s—since both models had been used in the war they were well known to the West. And as far as the training methods and number of personnel went—there were a number of technical advisors from the United States and the RAF occasionally visiting the academy, so surely this was not information that needed to be smuggled to the West. No, Josef told his interrogator, the whole situation at Karlovy Vary was nothing more than a botched romance. He had gone there out of uniform and walked with a cane because of a sprained ankle. Besides, wearing civilian clothes while not on duty was his right.

The StB man took notes as Josef spoke, and seemed satisfied with most of the answers he was getting. They went over the details of Karlovy Vary a few more times, and each time the questions were phrased a little differently to see if Josef would trip up. Finally the man called for the guards to open the door, collected his papers and put them in his briefcase and, with a nod and a small smile, left the cell.

But Josef's answers had not satisfied anyone. For not long after his first questioning, the guards entered again with another interrogator, and strapped Josef to the chair. The new StB agent, smaller in build, tried to force Josef to admit that he was involved with American Intelligence. Josef repeated his story. The man hit him. Without his glasses Josef saw sweeps of fists, blackness, bright pins. "You bastard," Josef said, through his swelling face. "You can do better than that."

"Understand something," the new interrogator shouted at him, close to his ear. "If we beat you to death nobody will know how your life ended. We will throw you in a grave and no one will know where it is."

My father has not told me about all of his initial prison experiences, and I suspect that he was beaten more than he wishes to tell me. I know that the charge of treason hung over him through most of his stay. After a period of two months, he was brought to the military prison at Hradec Králové. This place was far different than the underground prison of the StB: strictly grounded in codes of military ethics, prisoners here were treated like human beings. It was like breathing fresh air after the dank, deadly stay in the StB vault.

True to their word, Josef's friends at the Air Force Academy had told his family that he had been arrested. First informed by the Communists that he had been sent to Moscow as a prisoner of the Soviets, my grandmother somehow found out that her son was now in this military prison. When she came to visit him with Mira, and asked the military prosecutor in charge of the case what her son had done wrong, the man told her quietly, "Nothing criminal, mother. Nothing criminal."

Barbora and Mira were allowed to see Josef. He had lost weight and his skin, always brown, was now bruised and sickly white. They told him the family would do everything possible to get him out.

The relative peace of the military prison was short-lived. Soon, at the order of the StB, Josef was transferred to Pankrác prison in Prague, a former prison of the Gestapo, and at this time a kind of execution and torture factory. Here in interrogations prison guards were known to kick prisoners repeatedly in the groin, until death, and sometimes they placed a metal bucket over the prisoner's head and beat it constantly until the prisoner was driven insane. Pankrác was the primary political prison of the Communist government, filled to capacity with former democratic leaders, high-ranking military and police officers, leading intellectuals, priests, and ordinary men and women who had been courageous enough to publicly oppose the authorities. Three years later, in 1952, it would be at Pankrác that the famous Slansky show trial would take place, during one of the most dramatic Stalinist purges in Communist history; between 1949 and 1952, twenty-seven thousand political prisoners would see the inside of these walls. Most would be shipped to hard labor camps, a slow death sentence: more important political prisoners were executed, by hanging, on the Pankrác grounds.

Josef was put in cell number 64, on the second floor of the prison. He shared the small space with three others: a dentist whose father had been a member of the democratic parliament; a lawyer who was crippled—his knee had been broken during interrogation; and another man, named Ruda, who the others were suspicious of, because he was a friend of one of the guards in their section. The friendship did carry its advantages, however: the group was allowed to play cards and smoke cigarettes occasionally, acts that were forbidden in other parts of the prison.

On the heavy wooden door of their cell, a Gestapo prisoner had once scratched a message deeply with a nail. *Believe in the future of your nation*, it read, *and believe that your suffering is not in vain—1944*. Below it, a prisoner of the Communists had recently inscribed in similar fashion: *But it sure as hell was in vain—1949*. There was one small, iron-barred window high in the cell. In the center of the prison was a clock which rang its bell on the hour. On the nights before hangings the hourly chiming of the clock would cease—a silence to terrify the condemned in their last hours of life.

A week into Josef's stay, the door of cell 64 opened and a prison guard ordered Josef to follow him. They walked through a maze of corridors, and then into a section of the building which no longer resembled a prison: doors opened to executive offices with deep carpets and expensive furniture.

Josef was led to a door which read, "State Prosecutor." Inside, a young man, impeccably dressed in a dark business suit, sat behind a large desk. There were two chairs facing the desk, but Josef was not asked to sit down.

The State Prosecutor stood. He was tall and he glanced briefly at Josef and then down at a piece of paper before him.

"You are Lieutenant Josef Hůrka, of military unit 54-36." It was more of an accusation than a question.

"Yes," Josef said. He purposely excluded the customary addition of "sir."

"Born on August 9, 1925, in Radnice, of Rokycany county."

"Yes."

Reading from the page, the State Prosecutor charged him with the crimes of high treason and espionage for the United States of America. Each of these crimes, for an officer on active duty, was punishable by death. Josef was told he was an enemy of the Czech people, and that he had interfered with the great cause of socialism and conspired against the people's "democratic" regime in Czechoslovakia. He had, the man read, worked in the service of American imperialists to restore capitalism, and threatened the independence of the country. When the man was finished he looked up, glancing at Josef as if looking at a piece of wood, and called for a guard to remove the prisoner from his office.

Back in cell 64, Josef's cell-mates reacted to the

news grimly. Somehow their serious, drawn faces communicated the danger he was in more forcefully than the State Prosecutor had. Any time now, he might be told that his day had come to appear in court. There, after listening to the obligatory frame-up of false evidence (including that which they planned to force him into admitting during interrogations), he would be sentenced. He would be put into solitary confinement until his execution. He did not know how they informed you of when that would be.

On the first floor of the prison, in the hallways outside the interrogation rooms, those about to be questioned were forced to stand in a line with their noses against the wall and not speak to one another. Josef stood in these lines beside other patriots: priests and military men, professors and ordinary working citizens. At one point, he glanced to his right to see Dr. František Borkovec, whose brother Zdeněk, the former non-Communist Chief of Criminal Investigation for the Prague Police, had been one of the first on the scene of Jan Masaryk's murder. The Communists were cleaning up the "loose ends" that could be used to implicate them in the Masaryk killing, and this man was apparently one of them.

"I am sorry for what is happening to you," Josef told him, quietly.

"Not for me, son," Borkovec told him, "but for our country." He was hanged soon after.

Each day, from the exercise yard where the men walked for one hour, the prisoners waited to see if coffins would be driven out of the prison. When the prison hearses went by, the men watched them silently through the iron bars and barbed-wire fence. Afterward, in cell 64, Josef's cell-mates hoisted him up to the window where he could look down on the exercise yard of the condemned and report on who had survived the most recent killings.

During this time, my grandmother made constant pilgrimages to Pankrác. Once a week, she was allowed to bring clean laundry, some food, and some necessities to the prison for my father. He never saw these items. The prison guards, searching through my grandmother's carefully-packed box, would pull out toilet paper and make a game of throwing it around the room. *Pick it up, old woman*, they would tell her, laughing.

Many women came to Pankrác to try and give supplies to their loved ones. On the tram home with them one day Barbora said, "It's so terrible. What can we do?" Some of the women told her about a Communist lawyer who specialized in representing men accused of treason and espionage. Barbora went to him immediately, and for a down-payment of one-thousand crowns, his firm took the case.

Meanwhile Josef, despite the grim forecast for his future, tried to maintain his spirit. But Pankrác never let you forget where you were, and even in the exercise yard there were always reminders of what was going on in the buildings nearby. During their hour outdoors, the prisoners were required to walk in three concentric circles. In the outer circle, the younger, healthy men walked: in the middle were the older men who were more feeble, and in the center those who were crippled from torture moved as best they could. Political prisoners wore red armbands; regular prisoners who were incarcerated in Pankrác on work details wore yellow. The guards joked that this way, even if there was one day a revolution against the Communist government, when political prisoners broke out of Pankrác with their red armbands they would be killed by mobs thinking they were Communists. It would be, the guards said, a final Communist justice.

Josef lived a pendulum-like existence, swinging from weariness to terror, from the boredom of his cell and the brief air of the exercise yard to the sporadic interrogations. Throughout beatings and harsh questioning, throughout sessions where StB men shifted gears and pretended to be "friendly" to throw him off balance and trip up his story, he remembered something the sympathetic military prosecutor at Hradec Králové had told him, just before he'd been sent to Pankrác. *"You are a young man,"* the man had said, *"and obviously you have strong nerves. Even a State Court will not be able to convict you if you do not break down."* Josef had decided then and there that he would stick to his simple story of the truth, no matter what the interrogators did to him, and he would fight to live.

The Communist lawyer did little more than take the family money, and proved no help at all. But Josef's stubbornness during the questionings paid off. Entering his last interrogation, he was surprised to find a middle-aged StB man, alone, whom he had never seen before. The man sat at a desk, and Josef stood before him. There were no guards there ready to strap Josef to a chair—no preparations, that he could see, for a beating. The older man looked relaxed, and even fatherly. He pulled a sheath of letters from his briefcase, and read a few of them aloud to Josef. They were written by men in the military who had accused Josef of everything from laziness to insubordination.

"I hardly remember these people," Josef said.

"They couldn't have known such things about me, even if they were true."

The StB man shook his head sympathetically. "When you're down," he said, "some people will really prove to be bastards. It's crazy, isn't it? In these days, anybody could wind up in jail. This year it is you. Perhaps next year it will be me." He cleared his throat. "Mr. Hůrka, I think I can tell you what will happen to you from here."

The StB was now of the opinion, the man said, that Josef had not done the things he had been accused of, and the charges against him would likely be dropped. "But you'll have to be sentenced to something," the man said, smiling and shaking his head. "The Party cannot admit a mistake."

The meeting, far from being reassuring, mostly made Josef suspicious. What would happen to him now? For three weeks, he waited. Then, suddenly, he was cleared of the charges of treason and espionage and transferred to Loreta prison, near Hradčany castle. It was August, and looking out the prison truck window en route to Loreta, he saw people walking freely in the streets and the lush leaves of the trees over the sidewalks. He told himself to be grateful that he was not leaving Pankrác in a coffin, as so many others had. At the new prison he was brought before Lieutenant Praege, the warden, a man with an abnormally large head and strange flat eyes that were chilling. Josef had the thought that there was something horrible and disturbed about the man, and decided he did not want to visit an interrogation room with him. He soon found out from his new cell-mates that his instincts were correct: Praege, nicknamed the "dried up maple" by the inmates for his tall, ungainly shape, was a notorious sadist who enjoyed torturing prisoners in the Loreta cellar, viciously beating them or attaching electrodes to their genitals to shock them during questioning.

Josef was assigned to the upper floor of the prison. There, he was crowded into a cell with four others. Each day, for one-half hour after lunch, the inmates were required to read the State newspaper *Rude Pravo*, (*Red Right*), a silly litany of Communist bravado that at least was amusing. There were also two dog-eared copies of Communist-approved literature in the cell. On one of his first days in Loreta, Josef turned over one of these and found it to be *For Whom The Bell Tolls*. He read the book with relish: during his seven months in the prisons he'd had little to read, and Hemingway's tale of Robert Jordan and Maria fortified him, and took him away, if only briefly, from the sadness and horror around him.

He did not undergo any interrogations at Loreta. Because it looked like he might soon be released, some of his cell-mates made him promise that he would visit their relatives with messages, a commitment that he would keep for each of them.

Six weeks later, in a Loreta kangaroo court, Josef was convicted of five minor crimes to justify his incarceration. A parade of witnesses he did not know testified against him, knitting together a carefully rehearsed mesh of evidence. During his sentencing, he stood before the three Communist judges, their podium elevated above him. Behind them was a sign which read in huge letters: THERE WILL BE NO MERCY FOR TRAITORS. In front of them, centered on the podium, was a crucifix. It was a strange juxtaposition of images to watch as you were being judged. Josef was sentenced to five months in prison: since he had served nearly eight, he was released three days later.

His career in the Air Force was over. He had little chance of work, for very few employers would take on someone who had fallen out of favor with the Communist government. But none of that mattered much, for Josef was a changed man. One emotion consumed him when he thought of the people who had held him, and who now held his country, hostage.

He was furious.

Grandfather Josef's card to his Barbora, 1915.

CHAPTER FIVE

A HOSPITAL STORY

$\mathbf{M}$uch of what subsequently happened to my father I did not know until a December night in 1994, eighteen months after my return from the Czech Republic. I was visiting him in a hospital in Rutland, Vermont: a few days before, racing a friend down a trail at the nearby Killington ski resort, he had taken a hard fall. He had been knocked unconscious, his face was scraped with many cuts, and he had broken eight ribs. A doctor in Rutland who initially examined him failed to recognize a small, blackened area near his ankle where he had wrenched some skin. An infection had spread quickly and my mother had driven him to the Rutland Regional Medical Center, where he had been admitted and immediately hooked up to an IV for heavy doses of antibiotics. Now, three days into his stay, the immediate danger of amputation was past, and the blackness, slowly, was receding from his leg.

It was bitingly cold and as I walked into the Center

I rubbed my hands quickly together. I went through the main doors to the elevator, and punched the button for the fifth floor. Where I got off the hallways smelled faintly of antiseptic, and nurses were working diligently behind the main counter. I turned the corner and then turned in again a few steps to the left, into my father's room.

My father greeted me with a broad smile. I realized now, as I shook his hand, that I had never in my life felt like an imposition on him. He had always been glad, and even *grateful* to see me, and thinking back over my teen-aged years that seemed remarkable. He looked up at me happily. The IV was connected to his arm: they had just put it in, so it would remain there another half-hour or so. He had a white blanket over his legs and the television above him was off. He looked as though, before I'd come in, he'd just been sitting there, thinking. I pulled up a seat near him.

It was about seven-thirty, and our conversation was punctuated by nurses' voices over the intercom and an occasional visit from a strange but friendly orderly who scurried about, checking on my father's IV and leg, his movements like a squirrel. We joked about the accident and talked about my work at Tufts and Emerson. After a while our discussion swung to the writing I was doing about my Czech trip. I had heard bits and pieces of my father's skupina work throughout my life, and I knew that later he'd worked as a spy for American Intelligence, but I'd never been able to chronologically fit it all together. To make the book any kind of success I'd have to get some sense of it, I said. My father nodded agreeably.

"We can do it. Maybe we can do it here." He lifted

up his arm with the tube in it. "I have nowhere else to go." I pulled out some paper and a pencil.

I knew he couldn't tell me about his work in the nineteen-fifties with the American government, for he had taken an oath not to. All I could know about that time with any specificity was that what he'd done for American Intelligence was a continuation of his fight against Communism. But he could tell me about that time between his release from Loreta and his escape from Czechoslovakia. I had the sense that my journey to his old country and my interest in his story had opened a door for him—a part of his life that he'd always worked to camouflage was now being brought to light.

Through a friend, a lawyer, my father told me now, he was connected soon after his release from prison to a man who ran a Prague skupina. The nerve center of the group was located at the man's construction-contracting offices, off Bartolomějska street, very close to the StB headquarters. The resistance group specialized in bringing important statesmen and information out of the country and into the hands of United States Intelligence over the West German border. Though the nucleus of the skupina consisted of only a handful of professional people—lawyers, architects, secretaries, and members of the military—it was part of a large underground network.

"You made it a habit in this work to know as little as possible about those working with you," my father told me now, "so that if you were caught and interrogated you could not compromise them. You very rarely knew their real names. My code name was 'Vlasta.' "

"Vlasta?"

"In Czech, it could be a girl or a boy's name," my

father said, smiling at his younger, clandestine decision. "I took it from an old girlfriend."

"I remember her," I said. Some time before, on an autumn afternoon on my parents' porch in Brandon, my father had brought out a box of old pictures for my brother Chris and me to see. We had come across a picture of a pretty young woman in native Bohemian dress. On the back of the photograph, in Czech, the girl had written: *You can wait for your ship. Love, Vlasta.* Though he'd admitted the mutual crush, my father had been unable to remember what his girlfriend's message had referred to.

"Anyway," my father said. "The skupina took me on and I lived between three safehouses in Prague and a state farm on the border, in southern Bohemia. The director was with us and I stayed there when I was doing work in the area. I was paired up with a forester we knew as 'Pišta.' He was a good man, Joe, and courageous. He had remarkable vision, even at night, and he knew every inch of those forests on the border."

We had talked of Pišta before and I knew of Pišta and my father's mission to help Dr. Josef Macek and his wife, Běla, escape from the country. The sixty-two year old Macek was a leading political figure in democratic Czechoslovakia, and had been a member of the Czech Parliament before Hitler's takeover of the country. A close personal friend and advisor to President Masaryk, Macek had since 1923 also been the editor in chief of *Nase Doba (Our Era)*, a political journal which Masaryk had founded. In 1949 Macek was Professor Extraordinarius and Professor Ordinarius of Economics at the Technical University in Prague. He was known as a fierce anti-Communist and a leading contender for the presidency of a new, democratic Czechoslovakia. The Communist government feared his escape because he had the ability to unite Czechoslovak factions in exile and lead them against the Party—the same role Tomáš Masaryk had played against the Habsburgs during the First World War.

As the Communists slowly subjugated the nation, Macek was close to imprisonment. (A few months after this December interview with my father, Macek's son, George, now living in British Columbia, would tell me how close to jail his mother and father had come. "The day after my mother and father left," he told me, "the StB showed up to arrest them. Their neighbors repeated what my mother and father had told them, that they had gone on a ski holiday on the border of Poland.")

The escape of Dr. and Mrs. Macek took place on 19 December, 1949. My father described it for me in detail for the first time now. The skupina had asked Macek and his wife to board a train in Prague, and to dress as if they were simply going on vacation in Františkovy Lázně, a spa near Cheb, on the border of West Germany. They had been provided with false documents of passport for the Czech railway. Josef and Pišta boarded the same train in Prague and shadowed the older couple for the entire journey, hoping the Maceks would not be stopped. They were not: the train went through Kladno, Rakovník, and Karlovy Vary without any police searches. It went on toward Františkovy Lázně. At Nebanice, two towns before Cheb, the four travelers stepped off at a small station and the train hissed into the night, billowing steam. Six or seven commuters near them disappeared into the foggy evening. Pišta said to the professor, "Follow me, sir."

They walked to a darkened, abandoned building that had once been used as part of the depot. Dr.

Macek was tall and distinguished, carrying a single briefcase with his most important papers. Bela Macek was grandmotherly, and when she looked at you the sincerity of her eyes made you trust her immediately. They went in through a broken door and Pišta, briefly, shone a small flashlight around the cement room. It was empty, save for a small pile of bricks in one corner. Josef said, "Dr. and Mrs. Macek, I am Vlasta and my friend here is Pišta, our guide. We shall escort you to Germany. Before we start on the journey, Pišta will give us some instructions."

Pišta outlined what would follow. They would be hiking for about six hours. During the first two hours, before they got into the Šumava mountains, the Communists would check their papers if they were caught and would probably arrest them. After that, for the rest of the trip, they would all be shot on sight.

"The Maceks certainly were aware of the gravity of the situation," my father said, "but we could see that their faces were steady. This was a hard thing for them, their lives upturned and now this danger which they could not avoid. They were very, very brave people."

Josef and Pišta each carried two Fabrique Nationale (FN) 7.65 mm Belgian pistols with seven shots to a clip; Pišta told the Maceks that he and Josef would fight and give the couple a chance to run if they were halted by the *Pohraniční Stráž* (PS) border guards. If the four of them were *not* stopped on their journey, and made it to West Germany, they would still have to be careful, for West German guards (*Grenzpolizei*) on the take would still hand over escapees to the Communists. There could be no stopping to rest, Pišta explained. If they were to slow up for any reason, they would not make it to the border by morning.

"Then we all wished one another good luck," my father told me, "and we got started."

An hour into the trek, approaching a highway, Pišta, the Maceks and Josef dropped to the grass when they heard the throb of a motorcycle coming up the road. It was a Communist police patrol, and the bike passed by them harmlessly, the rider a solid rectangle tilting by some pine trees and then out of sight.

The group kept walking and after another hour they were in the danger zone. The mountains loomed around them, the large slopes sometimes glowing as the moon brushed through clouds. The Bohemian forest that the travelers entered was thick with trees and dark, and Josef was grateful for Pišta's night vision. The wind blew steadily from the west and they could hear the hum of the Marktredwitz electrical plant, twenty kilometers away in West Germany.

In the hospital room as my father told it all to me I could see the journey through his eyes: Mrs. Macek moving before him, her shoulders resolute, and before her the tall figure of Dr. Macek and more distantly, the moving shadow of Pišta. The forest floor and the mountain fields were a combination of snow, puddles and mud, and it was cold and raw. Sometimes, at the edge of snowy meadows, they could see footprints where the border patrol had just been. Though the skupina knew the patrolling routes of the PS, some seven hundred (six companies) strong in this area, they were never certain of PS routines or schedules, which changed on a daily basis. The hikers moved on carefully in their loose formation, never speaking.

The mountains grew more steep and they had to weave in-between large boulders. Josef and Pišta wore hiking shoes with rubber soles, but the Maceks, in city dress shoes, had more difficulty on the slick, snowy ground.

Then, in a rock cleft between two steep slopes, four hours into the journey, Pišta and Josef looked down on a snowy area with the fresh imprints of many boots. They had to get through the area, and through a gap at the end of it between two rock walls that opened up to a field. But were there PS guards waiting just beyond the gap?

There was no way to find another route and stay on their schedule, and so Josef would stay behind with the Maceks until Pišta checked it out and returned for them. Pišta left, and after too much time had passed Josef grew concerned. He told the Maceks to stay where they were and slowly he too went below, into the gully, slipping on the slick snow even in his hiking shoes. It was extremely dark in there and as he tried to regain his balance he pitched over a barrier of boards that the Communists had set up as a trap. The clattering was so loud he was certain the whole world had heard it. He stayed still in the snow, holding his breath. He looked up to the rocky gap where Pišta had disappeared. A shadow was coming. It grew and Josef raised one of his pistols. But the shadow materialized as Pišta motioning that everything was fine, and Josef lowered the gun and his shoulders and breathed deeply.

An hour later, from exhaustion, Běla Macek finally couldn't go on.

"Couldn't we break and rest for thirty minutes?" Dr. Macek whispered. "It's too much for her."

"If we break for that long we'll never make it to the border by daylight," Pišta said.

"I can take her," Josef said. He carefully took Mrs.

Macek onto his back, and they continued. He could hear the woman's exhausted breathing close to his ear.

"I worried constantly," my father told me, remembering. "She was a high target and anyone watching us would see her easily. I was always tense and determined to get her to the ground fast if I heard shots."

After some time, Běla Macek walked on her feet again, leaning heavily on Josef for support. He admired her ability to push herself through the fright and fatigue. Slowly, they wound down to the river Ohře that divided West Germany from Czechoslovakia. There was a small bridge ahead of them that Pišta had told them about, and an old stone mill farther in the distance that was now used for a PS barracks. The mill was a smudge of white in that early morning hour, and the wooden bridge arched over the icy water. Pišta went over quickly first. Then Dr. Macek. Then Běla Macek, with Josef close to her side. On West German soil they walked quietly in the same formation until Josef could smell gasoline: there, over the next ridge, on a small road, waited a long black limousine driven by an American operative. The four travelers got in and Josef rested his head against the back seat. Dr. Macek opened his briefcase and offered everyone a stash of apples. Beyond the operative and Pišta, out the windshield, it was starting to snow.

Our quick-moving orderly came into the room and, swapping jokes with us about my father being a practice pin-cushion for the student nurses, removed the IV. When he had gone my father pulled the sliding tray-table over, handed me some magazines and a book to clear away, and reached for my pencil and paper.

Slowly, he started to draw the diamond of Bohemia, and east of it Moravia and Slovakia. Then he concentrated on the western border with Germany, showing me the Czech city of Cheb, the German cities where there were safehouses, the height of the mountains, and his routes with Pišta.

"We spent Christmas of 1949 here," he said, drawing a small dot just over the Czech border, "in an American safehouse just outside of Bishofsgrün." It was my father's first Christmas without his family, and later, going over some of his written notes for this narrative, I realized how sorrowful a time it must have been for him, after the loss of his father only a few years before. *Now my mother and Mira were gone too,* he wrote to me. *I knew that I would not be able to contact them for a long time, for their own safety. They were alone, and exposed to the whims of a vicious political regime. At that time, however, we were still full of firm but naive hope: we believed we would defeat Communism within a few years—three, four at the most—and that Czechoslovakia would again join the ranks of free, democratic states. This may sound foolish today, but that was our goal at the time, and we were willing to risk everything for it.*"

He spent a lot of time hiking and running in the forests near the Bishofsgrün safehouse, trying to rebuild his constitution: he was still weak from his time in prison. Then, in late January, he and Pišta received word that the skupina needed them back in Prague. They waited for weather that was favorable to make their crossing into Czechoslovakia: clouds to assure darkness, and rain to hide the sound of their footsteps.

"Coming back *in* to the country that time was more of a problem than getting the Maceks *out*, really," he said, as I settled back into my chair, looking at his map. "We started to go back on the Macek route, only to find PS guards blocking the bridge."

Somewhat recklessly, instead of abandoning their journey at that late hour, they decided to try another route to the southeast, beginning near the village of Waldsassen. But it was 9:30, and they had hoped to make it to the abandoned railroad depot building by 3:30 am—leaving them an hour and forty-five minutes as a cushion against delays and time to shave and change into fresh clothes for a 5:20 commuter train. Their "cushion" would now be very thin. They swung their small, weather-proof rucksacks into the car of their American operative again and got in. It would take an hour and a half to get to Waldsassen, putting the start of their journey at about 11 pm.

The Waldsassen route had a number of snowy, open fields to cross: this too was a danger, for they would be exposed on that moonlit whiteness if the clouds lifted. They looked out the windows at the rain and the dark sky and prayed that the weather would continue to cooperate.

It did not. By the time they were in the Šumava mountains, the clouds were blowing across the stars. Then, as they crawled across one large field, the moon came out brightly. "We just stayed still in the snow, hoping if any guards saw us they would think we were rocks," my father said. "Pišta next to me kept cursing and saying he wished he could shoot the moon down."

After a while, when some darkness returned, the men made their way carefully about one hundred yards toward the forest. As they reached it they looked up and saw, just under the trees, a cigarette being raised to a face.

They lay dead still in the snow. After the cigarette

had gone out and a sufficient amount of time had passed, they crept to another side of the field. When they finally stood up, there were prints of border patrol boots all around them.

They struggled now to make up time. On a remote road, as they neared Nabanice and the sky was lightening, they suddenly came upon two factory workers who were on their way to work. The workers looked at Josef and Pišta strangely. The skupina men, talking softly to one another, debated incapacitating these factory men, for surely they would report that two strangers, their clothes muddy, had come *in* from the danger area. But Josef and Pišta finally didn't have the heart to do anything to the workers, no matter what risk came of it, and the workers passed them and continued up the road slowly, occasionally staring back.

Josef and Pišta had just enough time to throw on their clean clothes at the abandoned depot building and get onto the train as it left the station. They planned to go to Karlovy Vary and there catch a bus to Prague, but a few stops down the line a conductor told them, hazarding a guess at who they were, "I'm supposed to keep an eye out for two men, and to tell the StB if I see them, because apparently they are with the Underground." Then the conductor leaned down close to them, and said: "But to hell with the StB. I'll be damned if I help those bastards."

Josef and Pišta got off the train at the next stop, hiked north to a small village, and found a bus there that finally took them to Prague. "We felt it was some kind of miracle we'd made it there," my father told me.

In Prague, of course, my father was much more at home. He slept now in its shadows, shuttled from safehouse to safehouse, always with a constant supply of money that had been funneled to the skupina by American Intelligence. Watching my father talk about it this night, I remembered a story that Mira had told me, about how she and her brother and father had once been staying at Uncle Leo's flat as children and, one evening, aged ten, Josef had been admonished by father Hůrka for coming home late. *We thought you might be lost*, my grandfather had said. *Oh, I'm never lost*, Mira remembered my father saying. *I just watch for buildings and things on my way out and then keep them on my other side on my way back.* Mira said that her father had looked impressed at this. I thought of what an advantage my father's knowledge of Prague, and his sense of navigation under these later, difficult circumstances, must have been.

In March of 1950, Pišta and Josef traveled again by train toward the West German border. There in the abandoned depot building they met another government minister and his family: this time there were two children along. The children were drugged so that they would sleep through the night.

A little later, in the forest overlooking medieval Cheb, a city of about thirty thousand, Pišta stood beside Josef, looking down on the carpet of lights, and told Josef he had to meet someone there. Josef had not been made aware of this, and some intense, whispered debate followed. Pišta was carrying armaments production information from the Ministry of Industry, and it had to remain on his person, for he had the best chance of the two of them of escaping from this area if they were discovered. Finally, Josef decided to go into the city with him: they told the minister and his wife to stay in the forest, and if there was any commotion in the city below to head back to the trains.

Soon Pišta and Josef walked side by side through the ancient city streets. In this age of Communism, Cheb was largely deserted in the evenings: a woman shut a door here, looking suspiciously at them, and two old men gossiped at the next corner, giving them a quick once-over and then turning away. They went through a number of old squares cluttered with gabled and red-roofed houses. Birds scattered from the eaves. Josef tried to remember landmarks. Here at the Cheb Town Hall, he remembered, the general Wallenstein had been assassinated in 1634 during the Thirty Years' War. Here in another plaza was a clock to fix in his memory; nearby was a shop advertising shoes, and one block down a home with a garish coat-of-arms above the doorway. He was uneasy. He did not like the feeling of not knowing the area.

But Pišta knew where he was going. They came to a more modern building, dim white in the gloaming. The double-door entrance was dark and wooden and rounded off at the top. Inside, in the unlit foyer, Josef saw just enough to realize that there was some construction going on: a stairway wound around a large elevator shaft that was still without an elevator. They went up the stairs. At the third landing they stopped at an apartment door on the right. Pišta, with Josef to the right side and a step lower, touched the buzzer once briefly. Behind the glass window of the door, in what was apparently a prearranged signal of safety, someone's hand raised a candle and moved it in the form of a cross.

But the door flew open suddenly and the air exploded with the white fire of a sub-machine gun. Pišta's body, cut in half at the waist, slumped to the floor. The StB had not yet seen Josef and he took a few quiet steps down the stairs before flinging himself over the elevator shaft and onto the landing below. He sprawled, got up, and there were loud voices above. He took the stairs downward three at a time. As he reached the foyer, where the door was ajar, he briefly looked outside. Plain-clothed police were patrolling the front of the house. He ducked back into the dark hallway and found a door to the basement.

He went down wooden stairs. A single bulb at the bottom of the stairs lit the area. Josef's long shadow lurched against the strange contortions of dirt floor and rock walls. There was a heap of coal at a side of the room, and he thought for a moment about burying himself in it, and in the next instant imagined dogs sniffing, police laughing at the blackened man they had pulled from the coal. Then he saw a window.

It was a small window, granted. But it was partially open and Josef found a block to step on, shoved it over, and pushed the peeling window-frame higher and hoisted himself up and through, feeling splintered wood scraping his thigh. Now here was a yard, damp from an earlier rain. He smelled the dirt and someone's laundry, and he breathed hard and his shoes sank a little as he ran for the first fence. He clutched at the fence, scrambled, pulled himself over, twisted, and hit the ground running. Here was another apartment house. As he ran for the archway beneath the house a female voice from above was saying *Tamhle je, There he is*. He clattered through the hallway and onto a street, thinking bitterly that a great deal of people knew more about this rendezvous of Pišta's than he did. He ducked into an alley on the other side of the street and pressed himself against a cool stone wall, feeling his heart beating heavily as he sucked in air. A truck drove by close to him, dropping uniformed, armed police every fifteen feet, closing off the area that he had just escaped from. He started away from them, keeping to the shadows.

After one-half hour of seeing none of the landmarks he had so carefully noted along the way, he reached the outskirts of the city. He came to the bridge over the Ohře river that he and Pišta had crossed on their way into town. Several street lights cast faint light onto its wooden boards. He considered stripping and crossing downriver, where it was dark, holding his clothes atop his head. But he was exhausted, and not anxious for the numbing shock of the March water. He abandoned caution and took the bridge, feeling very alone and watching the dark smooth water move beneath him until he reached the other side.

"The minister and his family were sensibly gone," my father said. "My main worry was those papers on Pišta, because they would tip the Communists off about people who were working with us in the skupina."

I could place the rest of it, now, from stories Mira and my father had told me at different points in my life; my father ran east and north through the forest that night, following the river and the railroad. Near dawn, to cross the river again, on a railroad bridge where a sentry was posted, he waited for a freight train to come, then sprinted with it, using it to hide him and get him by the sentry. He tumbled down the embankment on the other side, then stuck to the forest again, following the tracks, until he came to a rural station where he watched shifts of guards searching for him. At an opportune moment, wedging himself into a group of commuters, he snuck onto the train and rode it back to Prague. The head of the skupina had already been arrested, but Josef was able to get to the home of another skupina member, whose personal letters, he knew, were on Pišta's body, and warn him before the StB arrived.

That evening he met with two other men, government informants, to warn them in person at a church on Vinohradská. The meeting had been planned for just after evening mass: my father and the two older men hoped to bury themselves in the crowd leaving the church. But something felt strange to Josef, as he looked at the church-going faces around him: some male faces seemed withdrawn, disconnected from the rest. He said to his companions, "Let's walk to St. Wenceslas Square."

They started down Vinohradská, openly followed by four StB men who came out of the crowd. Josef and the government informants kept a steady pace. Nearing the park at Wilson train station, using the cover of a tram car as it went by, they split up and ran: the StB, as Josef had hoped, chased him. He outdistanced the four men, but exiting the park on the other side two others in the long leather coats stepped out of the shadows with pistols pointed at him. He had run into a carefully-constructed ambush.

He raised his hands and watched the eyes of the StB man directly in front of him. When those eyes moved to see if he had a concealed weapon, Josef knocked the gun from the man's hands and, in a quick twisting judo motion, threw him to the ground. He jumped over the StB man and ran, zigzagging. He heard the snap of two bullets missing him. A third hit him solidly in the back, and his right arm went numb. He scrabbled for the FN pistol in his right trouser pocket and swung it to his left hand. He turned, fired a shot over the head of his nearest pursuer, and as the leather coats ducked for cover, he kept running.

The 7.65 mm bullet had missed his spine by about an inch, broken his collarbone and, over the next few hours, hiding in the streets of the Old Town, he struggled to stay conscious. At one point he dipped his head into the cold flow of a water fountain. It gave him life.

The safehouse that he had to get to was very close to StB headquarters. To make it there, he propositioned a prostitute at the edge of Bartolomějská street, walking with her by the StB building, looking, he hoped, like a disheveled drunk and keeping his bloody back away from her and from StB eyes. Across the street secret police moved in and out of the building frantically in their hunt for him. The prostitute rejected him just after he'd had enough time to make it by the StB post.

He made it to the flat and stayed there for eleven days, the bullet still in him, running a high fever from infection. He was tended to by an army general named Seydl, a concentration camp survivor now working with the Underground. The secretary who owned the flat gave them daily reports. An all-out manhunt continued for days in Prague, she told them: the Communists had found an overcoat, covered in blood, that belonged to a member of the Underground, and they were reporting that he was dead. It was my father's coat: he had abandoned it sometime after he'd been shot. Later, the Communists would bring the coat to my grandmother and Mira to prove that they had killed him. As a final insult, they told Barbora they would never let her know where her son had been buried.

My father was shipped through safehouses south and west, accompanied by Seydl: in a makeshift operation some fifteen days after the ambush, the bullet was finally removed late one night by a skupina doctor. Seydl and Josef stayed briefly at a farm in Hostomice, and then in Kladruby, near Radnice. From there, my father began a long hike out of the country. He was aided, initially, by his old girlfriend Vlasta, who had convinced her current boyfriend to drive food and clothes and shaving gear to Josef at three different points before the danger zone. That way, Josef hoped, he might simply look like a hiker if he were stopped and not like an escapee.

Much had changed in the border area since he had brought the Maceks to safety: the northern Šumava mountains were patrolled now by seventy-thousand PS troops. The Communists were quickly constructing a barrier of razor wire, sand, booby traps and mine fields. Watch towers had been built and armed with machine guns and searchlights, and the gunners told to fire at anything that moved.

My father walked south, where construction of the barrier was still under way and the mountains were sharper and considered more difficult to cross. In June of 1950, he went through the Bohemian forest and over the mountains of Czechoslovakia for the last time.

Mira had told me that at some point following this my grandmother had been admitted to an insane asylum. "I think she just needed someone to talk to," Mira had said. "She never knew anything about Joe's activities anyway, but she had been careful to never say anything to anybody that could get him in trouble. The actress in her needed contact with humanity. At least with the doctors she could speak, and not be afraid that anyone would take anything she said seriously. Who would really listen to her if they thought she was crazy?" Barbora would not see her boy again until 1964. The memory of his mother was too much for my father this night: I could see it in his face, and I swerved away from the subject.

Did he hear from the Maceks soon after? He had, he told me. A few days before Christmas, 1950, a letter came to "Herr J. Hůrka, Nueremburg, Hauptpost, Postlagernd, West Germany," a nondescript box address used by American Intelligence to transfer information to operatives. The name of the sender on the envelope was "Mr. J.M. Losman," the J.M. standing for Josef Macek. It was the start of a long correspondence between the two men, much of which focused on whatever up-to-date information my father could provide about their country: Macek, while on the faculty of the School of Business Administration at the University of Pittsburgh, was working with the Council of Free Czechoslovakia in New York, a Czech government in exile.

There was a postscript at the end of this first letter. *Dear Vlasta,* Mrs. Macek wrote. *We were happy to hear that you were successful in foiling the Communists' efforts to capture you. I am sorry, however, that our dear Pišta lost his life. Never, never will I forget that night. It was only because of your help that I was able to overcome the terrible stress and physical exhaustion—and then we parted company and I did not have a chance to thank you properly. I was so tired that I fell asleep immediately after I got in the car, and only as if in a dream did I hear when you got out. I hope that you will be able to come to this side of the ocean and start a new life. I think about you gratefully and with high regard. Yours, Běla Macek.*

The next seven years of my father's life will always

be a mystery to me. When I have asked if he worked with the CIA, he has told me that that is not precise: his participation was more military. "I was primarily gathering information," he has always said to my inquiries, his tone gently suggesting that the conversation end. He did not say anything more this night. I have always respected this familiar silence.

But I know a few details of this time, from brief things he has mentioned over the years, and from the scrapbook he assembled during the early nineteen-fifties that demonstrates the start of an avid interest in photography.

In the photographic album there are black and white pictures of the Tegernsee area of Germany where my father had a home provided by the U.S. government: these show a sparkling lake, and rugged mountains in the distance. Many breathtaking mountains are featured throughout the album, with captions alongside written in my father's steady handwriting: *Wilder Kaiser, Austria, from Walberg, March, 1952, Germany*, reads one, and *Garmisch-Partenkirchen, Spring 1953*, is inscribed by a set of others. Some photographs were apparently taken during ski trips: a number show a group of young people, perhaps from a ski club, laughing and talking as they ski, in file, through a snow-laden forest. My father is not in these pictures, and I assume he was behind the camera. He appears in some other shots taken later during camping outings and on the North Sea. There are also photographs of the various cars he drove: a military Jeep, a Studebaker, and a Mercedes, and sometimes there are pretty young women leaning against them, smiling. On the back of one such photo a woman has written something to my father in German, addressing him as "Pat." It occurs to me that none of the acquaintances featured could have known my father's real name. There are, too, pictures of seagulls in flight, and quiet winter woods.

The collection of album images is strange because its sense of normalcy contrasts with the life my father must have lived at this time to survive—a life without history, and without true identity. Only two pictures hint at his work. In them, he and another man are boarding a ship in a driving rainstorm: my father carries a suitcase, and you can hardly see his face behind the hood of his raincoat. They are on the northern tip of West Germany, and directly above them, in the North and Norwegian seas and up to the Soviet port of Murmansk, Soviet nuclear submarines are cruising back and forth, from the USSR into the western oceans. Though my father has suggested to me that he was involved with the investigation of Soviet nuclear submarine bases, I have no idea what, precisely, he did in this regard.

I know that he was held by no laws—if he was stopped by police in western countries, he produced staff credentials from the United States Headquarters in Heidelberg, Germany, that convinced officers to leave him alone. He presented himself as a U.S. Air Force Captain, a meteorologist, a Colonel in the Norwegian army. His work took him throughout western Europe, into the Soviet block, to the United States and frequently to England, where he bought British suits that he still occasionally wore when I was a boy. He carried two pills, apparently standard issue: one to keep awake, another cyanide. He disposed of both of them after a while, he joked with me once when I was a teenager, because he'd forgotten which was which.

When he came to settle in the United States the danger of Communist reprisals followed him, and he considered legally changing his name for good. He finally decided against it, omitted the krouzek mark (indicating a long "u" sound) from the original *Hůrka*, and otherwise kept his own name. He was given a villa in the Georgetown section of Washington, D.C., by the U.S. government, and offered a number of military jobs. He chose instead to work in the private sector, and moved to Beloit, Wisconsin, where he took a job as an engineer with the Warner Electric Brake and Clutch Company of Beloit, Wisconsin. He married, and I was born in November of 1960.

I knew things from there, he told me. He looked, suddenly this night, very tired. The clock above us read ten-thirty and the orderly came in to check on the leg. It still stunned me how black it was from about mid-calf on down.

"I hope the hell I'll be home for Christmas," my father said, looking angrily at his foot.

I told him I was sure he would (and this turned out to be true), and that he'd probably be skiing again by spring. The thought of it visibly brightened him. I shook his hand, holding back some emotion.

"Thanks for the talk, pop," I said. "I'll see you tomorrow."

"Ok, Buddy," he said, smiling, winking as he always does with both eyes.

Outside the cold got immediately into my bones. Despite the nagging antiseptic smell and the sterile hallways and aged patients all around him, I was glad my father was in warmth at that moment. I looked up at his window, where the light was still on. I started my Honda Civic and drove toward Brandon, and the stars over the mountains seemed close above me, like points of fire.

Young Josef Hůrka. "In family stories about my father there is a clear, steady thread of trouble running through his young life."

CHAPTER SIX

GHOSTS IN THE GOLDEN CITY

In the heart of the Old Town Square of Prague, or Staroměstske Náměstí, as it is called in Czech, is the Old Town Hall with its ancient astronomical clock. Every hour, crowds gather beneath the two great spheres of clock and calendar to watch the doors open at the top of the structure. There follows the mechanical march of eleven apostles and St. Paul, a display that has been playing forth since Columbus discovered America.

I met, on one day, Jana Pazlarová, an old childhood friend of Mira and my father's, now a tour guide at the Old Town Hall. Jana did not speak any English, and yet somehow, for a morning, we made do with a combination of pointing, some German, and some French. Jana first took me to see the old clock working from the inside of the clock-chamber, where we could see through the small windows the crowds looking up from the bright Square. I watched with fascination as the eleven apostles creaked their way about, led by St. Peter, on their small conveyor belt. Then the mechanical rooster above, outdoors, crowed, the clock struck the hour, and the crowd cheered. Watching this process from here, with Jana smiling next to me, I had the thought that the world Mira had offered me and the people she had linked me with was the sacred, inner world of Prague, a place that tourists could not easily look at, and I was grateful. I had been slowly realizing that my connection to Prague and this country was very deep and very intimate: I had started to feel this on my moments on the subway and in the shaded or golden streets—that the native faces I was seeing were strangely familial. This was more proof of it.

And then Jana took me up into the old tower, up the winding steps to the viewing gallery, where suddenly I could see the city below me. The wind was blowing hard there. Jana pointed out the sights to me: the National Theatre, where my grandmother once performed, by the Vltava, a magnificent green-blue rounded roof with golden spires coming from all four corners; the metronome on the hill, swaying in a kind of eternal timetable, built in 1991 on the spot where once a statue of Joseph Stalin stood. The magnificent Týn church that dominates the northeastern side of the Square was facing us: constructed in the latter part of the fourteenth century, it had been a focal point of the Hussite movement until 1620. High up across the river was Hradčany castle, now a beacon for me: often I could look up at the spires of St. Vitus to get a sense of where I was on my excursions. Many of the other sites that Jana showed me I could not identify, but I did not question her because it was quite difficult for her as it was, having to deal with someone who really knew no alternative languages to English, and I didn't want to complicate things for her even more. But I was thoroughly enjoying myself, looking at the great breadth of the city, at all the spires rising to the sun. And I perfectly understood Jana when she opened her arms wide and said, "Joe, *Prague*."

We went down again into the Square, by the Jan Hus monument with his exhortation to defend and serve the truth, unto death, frozen in stone beneath. Today, as most of the days I was in Prague, teen-agers flocked to the sculpture like seagulls do to rocks near the sea, basking in sunshine. There were mushroom-like fields of umbrellas put up for outdoor cafes on the Square here, many adorned with the red, white and black insignia of Marlboro cigarettes. Vendors sold postcards and magazines, Bohemian glass, and small wooden figurines of various political personages: Gorbachev and Bush, I could see, were quite popular still. Pigeons fluttered back and forth, from cobblestones to shadowed doorway eaves. There were ironsmiths at work on the square, hammering away with steam rising from their troughs nearby. Artists next to them were at work on portraits, rapidly turning a profit. Salesmen near buildings on the south side advertised abandoned Russian army paraphernalia—hats, buttons, badges, and coats, though I was later to find that the manufacture of "old" Russian hats and uniforms was a popular basement industry in some parts of Prague.

I did not know where Jana was taking me, though finally, when we turned onto a side-street and walked by an exclusive clothing store, Jana said the word "Mozart" and I realized that we were en route to the Estates Theatre where Mozart once performed. I had told Mira this was a place I really wanted to see. And here it was, Stavovské Divadlo in Czech, the building where the maestro gave his premiere of *Don Giovanni* in October of 1787, now a performance center for artists of all hues: opera, theatre, dance. The building is exquisite, light green with white and gold trim, in the neo-classical style, and was newly renovated.

I had always wanted to walk through doors where Mozart once walked, and now I did, and Jana and I met a curator who also spoke no English. Together, they gave me a private tour of the building. We went high onto the balconies where the lights were set up for the theatre below. Beneath us, at the lower point of steep, rich red seating, a theatre troop was busy rehearsing on stage. But I was imagining Mozart there, working with his musicians in that same space, two-hundred and six years before.

There was a discussion that was going on between director and actors that seemed exploratory and full of quick passion.

"Arthur Miller," the curator said next to me.

"I know this play," I said. "This is *Death of a Salesman.*"

We moved on, down into white, elegant reception rooms, then through a hallway and to a small sitting room. The room was very quiet, and pleasant, but Jana's eyes were wide as the curator moved toward a set of doors at the end of it. Jana touched my arm and motioned for me to follow. The curator opened the doors and I saw a shaded balcony with chairs that seemed dark in contrast with the bright light of the rehearsal beyond. We went forward and saw the actors moving just below us through the new routine they had been discussing. I looked down at the chair I was touching. It was covered with immaculate, shimmering blue velvet. Jana tapped it lightly with her fingers. "Presidente," she said. "Havel." Then I understood that I was in the presidential box.

On a hill just west of the Vltava river, at Mozartova 169, the villa Bertramka stands beneath a grove of trees. It is a seventeenth-century farmhouse that was refitted in the eighteenth century to blend with its more metropolitan surroundings. During the day in this early summer the vivid green of the leaves complemented the sprawling, relaxed, yellow and white structure. The gardens just beyond the house, up the hill, were thick with green, and you could almost believe that somewhere there, walking with a universe of creation going on inside of him, was Wolfgang Amadeus Mozart.

In the late eighteenth century Bertramka was the home of Josefína Dušková, an opera singer who had befriended Mozart in Vienna and invited him to stay at the villa she shared with her husband, the composer František Dušek. Here, shielded somewhat from the financial woes that dogged him throughout his life, Mozart spent some of his happiest days. He was much loved in Prague, and in this same garden pavilion he composed the overture to *Don Giovanni* hours before he would take to the stage with it at the Estates Theatre.

Mira and I bought our tickets and picked up guidebooks at the front door of the villa, now a museum to Mozart recounting his life and visits to Prague. Here, in rooms leading gently and formally into one another, were the things of Mozart: the interior with period furniture and a J.H. Grubner harpsichord which Mozart played, and Mozart's pianoforte which I touched with reverence. Here was his bedroom, still with its original ceiling, a multicolored affair that he woke to in the mornings; on the wall, facing the area where Mozart's bed once was, were two portraits: one of his son Franz Xaver and another of an unknown woman. She was dark-haired and very beautiful. I imagined Mozart looking at the bold, aristocratic face of this woman, and at Prague out the windows.

At the entrance again I bought a silk scarf for my girlfriend, Beth, and for my mother, a lover of classical music. Mira remarked on the beauty of the scarves—portraits done of the composer in purple and black and red with great flourish—and I made a mental note to surprise her with one before my journey was over. And then we went out the doors and walked together in the gardens of Bertramka.

Mira took me all over the city: to St. Nicholas Cathedral in Malá Strana (Little Quarter), where the first tribute to Mozart after his death was held, and to the Municipal House (Obecní Dům), a kind of mecca for students of art nouveau and the site on which, on October 28, 1918, Czechoslovakia was proclaimed an independent republic. She arranged for me to see the oldest chamber of Charles University, the Carolinum, dating back to 1348 when the King had determined that his place of education would be for all students, from in or out of the Bohemian kingdom. We saw Roman ruins beneath the city, and the gold and diamond-crusted liturgical collection from the sixteenth through eighteenth centuries at the Loreto monastery. I looked with wonder at manuscripts dating back to the ninth century at the Strahov monastery library near Hradčany castle, and visited the Rudolfinum, the Czechoslovak Parliament building between 1918 and 1939 and the current home of the Czech Philharmonic Orchestra. We walked through the Old Jewish cemetery beneath its canopy of trees where crows caw and fly; nearby I was stunned, gazing at the inner walls of the Pinkas Synagogue, where the names of 77,297 holocaust victims are inscribed.

I went through the National Museum on Wenceslas Square, and in the Pantheon of statues of Czech artists, writers, and scholars I stared up at the bronze figure of Tomáš Masaryk, his two fingers pressed together by his side in the symbol of truth. After a long trek another day, Mira and I walked through the Royal Gardens up by the castle, where her hip ached and my leg was giving me trouble, and we sat on a bench and joked that if we could just trade parts maybe we could get some relief. A few minutes before, I had taken a picture of Mira at the Gardens entrance for my father to see. After the Communists had taken over the country, the Gardens had been closed to all but Communist officials, and one of Havel's first acts as president had been to re-open these former playgrounds of Habsburg rulers to the public. At various points on the great lawns of the area the new, democratic government had posted signs in four languages that read *May Peace Prevail*.

I drew all of these things in, and let them stir in my blood. Gradually I spent a great deal of time simply walking alone through the city, sometimes having no idea of where I was. I loved the golden light slanting over its walls, its ancient, unending buildings, its trams clanging matter-of-factly through the streets. Prague was mysterious and profound and magical to me, and on days when I made these journeys, I jumped on and off trams with workers and city dwellers, feeling more and more a part of their fabric. In the city haze the stone sidewalks were filled with a river of commuters, and I joined that flow, all of us walking over the same ground our ancestors had one thousand years before.

Milan Entler owns the Entler-Dvořáková gallery, where Mira works, on Loreta Square. He has eyes that tell you he has seen many things. His wife, with whom he founded the gallery, has since passed away.

In the shop, a small, white room with track lights that somehow feels spacious and intimate at the same time, Milan shows Milena Dvořáková's work, his own, and that of other talented Czech artists. His building is perfectly situated at the southeastern tip of the Square, across from Černín palace, and to your left, as you look out the shop windows, you see the Hradčany castle spires. The area this May was constantly flooded with tourists. Behind the retail area is a small apartment that Milan occasionally stays in.

Milan had given Mira, as a gift for me, a sheath of Entler and Dvořáková prints. On the day that I met him at the gallery, about a week into my journey, I thanked him. Mira told him I was having some difficulty moving around because of my broken leg, and Milan nodded and disappeared into his apartment. He came back with a plastic bag full of colorful herbs. Mira translated his instructions for me: we were to mix the herbs with water and wrap them in a towel, and put it on my ankle in the evenings. It would reduce the swelling. Then Milan brought a glass of juice that he had made himself from berries he had grown on his farm outside Prague. I thanked him: the juice was delicious, and I asked him for a refill, thinking that he could market the stuff if he wanted to. We talked for a while about my visit and then Mira told him we were going to see the Loreta prison where my father had been held last. Milan looked at me with his deep eyes and nodded sadly.

It was just through the Square and a few steps down sloping Kapucínská Road behind the Loreto monastery. There was no one on the street and Mira and I stood before the gate where prisoners once entered and left. Here, forty-four years before, my grandmother had waited for her son's release. I imagined her standing there, waiting, and how she must have felt finally seeing him walk out. There is now a sign to the right side of the gate, on a pastel-pale yellow wall, that reads: *Památce obětí umučených komunistickou policií, In memory of those tortured to death here by Communist police.* When we walked a little farther down the street and looked over the prison wall, we could see the third floor window to the cell where my father had been held.

In the quieter, back-streets of Prague, sidewalks are swept and stores now have large windows; once Mira, as we were walking, told me that you did not see much of either of these before. No one bothered to keep the streets and sidewalks clean (and why should they have? There was no real incentive to sell under the previous government.) and storefronts usually had only a small window, rather than a large one displaying wares. Bars and other neighborhood eateries, too, had been spruced up to attract business. Though sometimes I am impatient with advertisements, I saw them here as a symbol of a healthy economy, and where the economy is free the mind usually is as well.

On the electric trams which hustled through the city—moving billboards with advertisements for cigarettes, clothes, electronics and a host of other products—there was a newer, more positive attitude between people that Mira told me she had not seen for many years: citizens were not afraid to speak and be kind. During Communist days, she said, these human sentiments and the collusion of humanity that they suggested were ultimately dangerous elements to the State, and they could land you in jail. The feeling *I* had, not only in these back-streets but also in the tourist areas of Prague, was akin to moving within the body of a giant who has carefully measured his breathing for too long, and now at last breathes freely and without danger or restriction.

Physically, many things seemed to be caught in between the two systems. The historic buildings which had been ignored and had fallen into disrepair under the Communist system were now being furiously renovated—many of these by the government, and many by private owners who had reclaimed the property taken from them by the regime. You would pass, on any given day, many buildings where high up on scaffolding workers were scraping or repairing or painting the stylish baroque architectures. And yet, at one point on a side-street, Mira and I passed two government workers who had apparently been digging up some pipes in a sidewalk. There was a gaping hole, some shovels stuck in the dirt nearby, and one of the workers, extremely fat, was sitting, and the other one was standing idly, and Mira told me they were talking about when they should stop working. I laughed and said "It seems like they already have stopped work," and Mira said "That's like it always was under Communism," and I thought, looking at them, that you might find them in many American cities as well, working for the city, just putting in their time.

Czech money, too, represented this period of transition: the Communist star still rose over the Bohemian lion and idyllic scenes of workers and students and heroes on bills and coins. When I was a teen-ager Mira had told me stories of how people waited with this money in lines, for a little bread, a little meat, for shoes that would not fit. I would be grateful, one year after my journey, when she would send me Xerox copies of the new currency, with no star over the lion.

At night, after long days of walking, I sat in my chair with my foot wrapped in towels doused with ice water and alternated these with towels bound around Milan's formula of herbs. As I waited for the swelling to go down, I wrote out scenes and impressions, moments and inspirations, gradually creating a mental mosaic of this time, in Prague, just after the revolution:

A girl, perhaps sixteen or seventeen, turns a corner, and walks onto Vinohradská Street. I watch her from the apartment window. Some older people, I am sure they are her parents, walk just behind her. The girl is dressed gaily, in a light brown sweater and a short, blue-patterned dress and heels. She has long, bare legs and moves with that sensual, non-aware wisdom that a young woman can have. Her parents, both dressed in a more severe blue, watch her and then each other, smiling. A tram with the giant words Coca-Cola written on its side rattles and whines electrically by and blocks my view a moment. Then I see the three of them going by me and up the road to the crossing, and the girl's brown hair dances over the back of her sweater. As she walks, her movement seems to be saying to her parents: look at this new, bright world you can walk in with me, just look at this world.

In the center of Wenceslas Square I stand at the Circle of Martyrs. Below me is the picture of Jan Palach; Palach and a group of fellow students had volunteered to become, one by one, living torches to the spirit of their country, but only Palach and another student one month later, Jan Zajíc, finally took their lives. The Masaryks, father and son, look out at me too, and I read plaques near them with homages and names of those who fell to totalitarianism. Across the background of all of this is the Czech flag, white, blue, red. And everywhere, as if put there by invisible hands, are flowers, in jars, as wreaths, or laying across the ground.

A German group of students watches the memorial. They are young, and their teacher speaks to them, explaining the various names and pictures and the lives they represent in the Circle. I notice that the wind has blown down two pictures. Feeling a little silly, but feeling also that it needs to be done, I move into the Circle and set the pictures aright. I have a strange moment beyond self-consciousness. What is it? I step out of the Circle. The German group leaves and oddly, then, there are very few people around me in busy Wenceslas Square. A second time the wind blows, harder, and I go to pick up more pictures and flowers that have fallen. And here it is again, in the Circle, a feeling that other lives are there with me, still deciding within that human labyrinth of will and fear and courage to do something symbolic and knowing that it will last in history but also that that does not matter: you are afraid, and fear consumes you. But you are here now, and the world is waiting for what you have lived all of your life to say. It is time to carry it through. I smell gasoline. I see flames. I put up small jars of flowers, the dirt a frightening, tangible thing close to me. I set the pictures up as firmly as I can and these ghosts are singing. I step quickly from the Circle.

I go across the avenue and to the sidewalk, into the crowd of pedestrians, relief moving through me after that moment alone in the strong wind. Here the sun comes down and I can smell many different foods on grills beneath the thick, low leaves of trees. Still, somehow, the sun gets through and there is light everywhere—and for a moment the fate of Jan Palach and Jan Zajíc seems so horrible. I understand a young woman tried to burn herself to death after the two young men did, but friends stopped her. I grieve for all of them, in this brightness, and for Jan Masaryk, that cultivated, wonderful man, thrown to his death in the darkness. It is too much, and I try to shake the grief. There are many nationalities together in this place and, for this moment, no one is threatened. Vietnamese vendors next to me sell newspapers. Shoppers move in and out of music, clothing and book stores. I hear French, German, Italian.

I walk a while. Then, of all places, I step into a McDonald's. Though the establishment is huge and cavern-like on this first-floor, there is a very brief line. It's early in my journey, and I'm not too handy with the money system yet. These are some quick young Czech McWorkers, capable of handling every language thrown at them. When I step forward to the tall, smiling young man in his McDonald's uniform, I smile apologetically and issue what is, by now, my standard line.

"I only speak English, I'm sorry."

"Is ok," he says.

"I'll have two cheeseburgers—"

"Cheeseburgers, two," he taps into the machine.

"And—frites?" This is my attempt to meet him half-way on the language thing.

"Frites?" he laughs. "You mean French fries?"

"And a Coke, medium."

"And a Coke," he says. "And would you like to do the apple pie this day?"

Now it's my turn to laugh. "No thanks," I say. He smiles good naturedly. "It is my duty to ask this, no?"

"In America too," I say.

He tells me my price, still smiling.

Upstairs I stare out the window at trees and through their green brightness at the avenue below. Two men are having an animated discussion down there that I cannot hear. I look at my tray liner: Mc-Donald's je už v Praze! it shouts at me. McDonald's has arrived in Prague!

I look out the window again. I think about all the times my father stepped through police doors and was nearly extinguished from history, and so too me, and the leaves outside, trembling with wind, seem to hold this fragile secret as well.

On one slightly overcast day, Mira and I went to see the church where the seven Czech parachutists made their last stand against Nazi SS troops. We descended from the tram at Charles Square, next to a park with many trees. Lovers sat beneath the beech and elms and the slight shadows of leaves moved over the grass. We walked in the wind across the Square and then across Resslova and along the buildings. From articles and pictures I had seen of the church, I expected it to somehow be standing alone, but here suddenly it was, just, at least from this angle, another building on the street with a narrow, horizontal window leading to the crypt. The window was still pockmarked all around the edges with bullet holes from the seven-hour standoff. There is a plaque above with names inscribed and a relief of a paratrooper on one side, his head lowered, and a priest on the other. The names on the plaque stand as a simple list of courage: *Opálka, Gabčik, Kubiš, Valčik, Švarc, Bublík, Hrubý.* And the religious men who aided them: *Gorazd, Čikl, Petřek.* I tried to fix them all in my head.

I thought of those last hours here: the sound of gunfire, the tear gas and grenades. Rushing water from firehoses to flood the parachutists out of the church; final shots as the water rose in the crypt. The courage and the horror of it all struck me now, standing here with my aunt in this quiet day.

"It was a day like this one, Joe," Mira told me. "I remember it. With some clouds, like this. They had roped off the whole area. Everybody knew that something big was happening."

On the high ledge beneath the plaque there were, everywhere, fresh wreaths and flowers and notes.

A while later I stood on the Jiráskův bridge where, forty-four years before, my father sometimes stood too, waiting and watching. There was a safehouse apartment across the river that he could sleep in at night, and Mira pointed it out to me—a large brownstone at the opposite right corner of the bridge. The flat belonged to a deputy minister of Industry who worked with the skupina, and if the coast was clear for my father the minister's wife would leave one curtain in an upper window folded back, so that he could see a triangle of light from the apartment. I had seen the bridge before on a postcard. I had not known then how close Mira's apartment was to it—a simple, fifteen-minute ride by tram. On the evenings in 1949 that he stood here, my father would not see Mira or his mother again for many years. They would not know if he were dead or alive until a letter—sent to them by a mutual friend some three years after his disappearance from the country—suggested cryptically (using an old nickname of his from childhood) that he was in England.

Sometimes my father had waited here, and now I knew why: trees gave fine shadow at the shore side of the bridge, and if he needed, quickly, to escape, he could have slipped back into the metropolis easily.

As we walked over the bridge and by the apartment building my throat was tight and I was full of emotion, and this was beginning to happen so frequently to me that I wondered if my trip and what I was doing on it was intelligent at all. It was as if I'd returned to a place of too many painful memories, though I'd never been here before.

I was able to shake it off some on our excursion of Petřín Hill above the city. The area had once been part of an orchard of the Strahov monastery and the flowers were not fully in bloom yet, Mira said, but they would be soon. She had loved this place since childhood, she told me.

There was a small shower and we stood under some trees, laughing, and waited it out. Then it lifted and we walked by the "Hunger Wall," a project that King Charles started in 1360 for the poor of Prague so that they would have honorable work and sustenance: some twelve hundred meters of the wall survive. At some points, going by it, I felt I was on the set of a *Robin Hood* movie: those ancient walls with slotted battlements were bordered by forest and grass, and I imagined medieval knights riding beneath them. The partial sun clouded over and the green of the forest shadows deepened.

And then it rained in earnest, and we ran again for the funicular railway. Our car ran on a slant down the steep hill with stairway platforms for passengers, and Prague, under rain, seemed to rise before us.

That night I wrote this:

I go to the church of the martyred priests and parachutists, and later to the bridge where Dad waited for the chance to sleep, sheltered, for the night. These two places are not far from each other. Today it is early spring, and warm, and flowers are starting to bloom. Everywhere you go in Prague there are young people, and they look bright and intelligent. The tram station and park at Charles Square are full of people waiting, and young lovers embracing. They embrace, they kiss with abandon. It seems fitting in this place of martyrs and fighters that there should be a spring day full of joy and young love. Looking at it, I feel I can hear the people who fought for this approving and applauding.

Mira, as a teen-ager, in native dress.

CHAPTER SEVEN

STONES AND CASTLES

The next morning Mira woke with a flu. She was angry at herself for getting it during the time I was there. I told her not to worry, and secretly I did not mind the thought of a few days unbound, on my own in the city, with Mira resting, for it had worried me the amount of walking she was doing. She called the doctor and arranged for a meeting, and it was set for the early afternoon, and I took the subway into Wenceslas Square to take some pictures. When I returned we walked the few blocks down Vinohradská Avenue to the clinic.

There are *clinics* in the Czech Republic, and these are mostly for outpatient services, and they are staffed primarily by female doctors, and the hospitals, as I understand it, are staffed mostly by male doctors. During the Communist regime the finest facilities—the hospitals—were reserved for the elite of the Communist party. Once, on the outskirts of Prague, I saw one of these Communist hospitals, a modern building set on a hill among trees. I was told it had been quite exclusive. I had the thought that it was remarkable how ably the leaders of the "worker's state" removed themselves, in treatment, from the workers.

This clinic was no such place. It was a small, white building, perhaps built just after the war, set in among other shops and apartment buildings. We walked by a few cars parked in front of it, two Volkswagens and a Czech "Škoda," and I assumed that these belonged to the doctors, who were not as highly paid as in America. Then there was a hallway that you entered directly from the outdoors with a set of doors and elevators. We took an elevator up to the third floor. The elevator was small and old, but efficient, and it let us off into a hallway that was wide and well-lit and with fading but clean tiling.

At the end of the hallway was the sitting room for two offices, one of these the one that Mira needed. The floor, here too, was of that old gray tile, and the benches were wooden. There was a set of windows that looked out onto the sunlit day, and two doors of blond wood. The walls were whitewashed and bright. We sat on a bench to wait: we were the first there of the afternoon. Then more Czechs came in, saying "Dobrý den"—a cheerful greeting or farewell—and the women doctors came in and opened their doors with their keys. Just before her appointment I told Mira I would go to the Olšany cemetery across the street and meet her when she was finished in an hour.

At the entrance to Olšany there was a woman selling flowers and I bought a rose, bringing out the only money I had, a two-hundred crown note, and the woman took the bill and went into her small shelter for change. A bird twittered above me and I looked into the shade at the dark monuments, and the woman came out again with my change and counted it very precisely into my hand. I thanked her and walked through the stone entrance.

I have never seen graveyards so carefully maintained or elaborate as those I saw in the Czech Republic. I was used to the rather austere, simple nature of American graveyards: it is not that unusual to see a grave in decay or untended in America. So these Czech stones, so close together and huddled beneath abundant greenery, many elaborately decorated with figurines of saints, seemed overwhelming at first. And yet there was a peace about this attention lavished on the dead, and I thought it would make all those living in a society like this have the feeling that they were important even after death, that even death could not still certain aspects of the spirit.

The inner graveyard walls contained urns set behind glass, with photographs of those whose remains were within. I looked at the long march of faces staring out at me, and I wondered how these people had managed, bound day to day by a philosophy that sought to dehumanize them, to oil them to fit into the Communist machine. Here were stories, too, beneath these dark, well-polished vertical and horizontal stones where one could see one's reflection like a ghost: here a man died, and beside him his wife died four days later; here were flowers stacked on a tomb, a candle flickering in the shadows, placed there obviously minutes before by some relative on this windless day. Then I came to the grave of Jan Palach.

It was, by these standards, a fairly simple monument. There is a headstone that says *Jan Palach*, and then the standard horizontal stone. On the horizontal stone there is a sculptor's rendition of a man. It is a long figure, in rough-hewn flat relief, as if the man, through some great trauma, is either raising himself from the stone or descending into it. But he has no features, and one has the feeling, looking at it, of extraordinary tragedy and sacrifice. The sculpture was put together after the revolution, Mira had told me: before that time, the Communists had discouraged pilgrimages to this grave. Later, I would read the chilling letter this student wrote before his death, in trying to alert the world to the Czechoslovak tragedy: *It was my honor to draw the lot number one/ and thus I acquired the privilege of writing the first letter/ and starting as the first torch.* As he'd burned, Palach had been heard speaking the names of Jan Hus and Jan Masaryk.

I put my flower next to some others at the head of the stone, and touched the stone. Then I walked out a side path of the cemetery into the sunlight.

At a nearby cafe I had a Coke and wrote in my book while I waited to go for Mira. This time I was writing a direct letter to my father, for lately I had been increasingly speaking with him in my head. *Dad*, I wrote, *let's put a final nail in the coffin of this thing forever. Let this experiment in bureaucratic power never be repeated. That is something worth fighting, and writing, and dying for.*

I read my words over, once, and looked out the window at traffic, at people walking by Olšany, and soon it was time to go back to the clinic.

That weekend I organized a tour of Konopiště and Karlštejn, two famous castles outside of Prague. I was as much interested in viewing the countryside of the Czech Republic as I was the castles.

Most seats were filled in our air-conditioned tour bus, and I had a vague feeling of guilt as we moved out of the city. Somehow, in the cool, soft, carpeted tourist machine I felt separated from the Czechs on the streets I was moving through: I had gone from the vibrant world of revolution and recovery to a seat of impartial observation. Near me was a loud American with a military crew-cut who was talking up the horrors the Czech people had endured through fascism and communism: apparently he had just discovered much of this information and was intent on sharing it with everybody else to get their reaction too.

"I was stationed in Germany," he was telling one uneasy French couple now, "and I never thought I'd see this place as a tourist. I thought we'd be visiting these Reds in our little green uniforms."

He was mercifully drowned out by our Czech host, an older, graying, bespectacled woman with a kindly face who spoke in both French and broken English over the bus intercom system. On our way out of Prague she pointed out some sights and spoke of their corresponding history, and on the outskirts of the city the future was in evidence: we swung by a large Mercedes showroom full of luxury cars, and across the highway there was a Ford dealer, with row upon row of the glossy American automobiles, and then we were on the open road in greener, rural areas, telephone wires rushing by, and I had my first glimpse of the world outside Prague.

Czech villages do not sprawl, as many American villages do: they are tightly-bound, so that one building often is connected to another and you see neighborhood after neighborhood this way, with old, stone streets, (indeed, it struck me once that the space of American towns might be a *reaction* to the tight form of European communities) and when you are clear of the town you see nothing but lush green, neatly-kept farmland or wild land, and rolling hills. Because I expected to see, after the Communist years, rural areas in terrible shape, I was pleased to find farms in the countryside in order; though many of them did not have the heavy machinery and elaborate buildings that I'd seen when I once lived in Iowa, they were nevertheless quite well-cared for, and clean, and the farmhouses were painted neatly.

Here were seas of green, and hills with wild grass above farms and towns, and it made me think of the Bohemia I knew from paintings in my home when I was a boy: skies of blue, fields of hay and wheat, and women in colorful dresses gathering crops. We passed people dressed in more modern fashion now, through a town where some women, standing together with children playing all around them, were talking; on a street above them a boy, perhaps ten, dressed in a soccer shirt and shorts, rode his swanky BMX bicycle, the sun glinting off his handlebars.

We sped again into grass country, and it was here, for the first time, that I saw the remarkable golden caps on the hills, the fields of the řepka flower that grows in such abundance and so thickly in Bohemia that it looks, from a distance, as if the hills contain some inner glowing light. I wondered: could these be the fields of legend, from which the ghost soldiers of St. Wenceslas rose to defend the nation? As I looked on, it seemed quite possible: I could imagine the ancient soldiers emerging from that brightness, so magical, so alive, seemed that golden light.

Roughly an hour outside of Prague we came to the castle Konopiště, which was originally built in the thirteenth century and renovated into a private palace by the Archduke Franz Ferdinand, heir to the Habsburg throne. The assassination of this Habsburg lord touched off World War I; later, Konopiště was used as a headquarters for the Nazi SS in World War II.

We walked up through a shaded forest of pines to the castle gardens, where one of our troop, a stunning, dark-skinned Italian woman in a light green dress, posed with a grounds peacock for friends' cameras. I watched the woman for a while and then went into the courtyard, where as we waited for our tour to begin we were told to browse through the gift shops. I bought a postcard in one of these shops from a pretty salesgirl, so that I could remember the place for my writing. The postcard showed an aerial view of Konopiště, the red-roofed cone towers rising over the forest and the carefully-tended grounds and a blue lake beyond. Soon enough, our tour guide came to meet us at the courtyard, and we began our excursion.

After the SS occupation, Konopiště had been restored to the state Ferdinand had left it in, with his rather eccentric collection of weapons, and a vast array of mounted animal heads on the walls—a fraction of the thousands of animals he killed in his lifetime. The effect of all this, on me, was immediately nauseating: here were weapons, floor after floor and a whole showroom of them, from ancient battles: a large executioner's ax (this one was built as a 'prototype,' our guide explained to us, and then purchased by Ferdinand, "and it hasn't been used—*yet*"), pistols and guns from the sixteenth century, a full-armor model of a knight on a horse, a set of dueling pistols behind glass that had once belonged to Napoleon, and rapiers and swords and muskets from various ages arranged and displayed garishly, each a subject of Ferdinand's reverence. An Irish woman from our tour kept describing the weapons as "lovely," a word I hoped came from a certain habitual use of language rather than her emotions.

I told myself, morosely, that I was walking in a house of death. To make matters worse, our American military expert was jawing his observations into the ears of anyone unsuspecting enough to listen. I thought of my grandfather in World War I, and of three hundred thousand men dying in a matter of days by the river Marne, and I wondered, why would anyone die for the honor of the pompous, bored idiot who inhabited these quarters? We were given ·a tour of Ferdinand's chapel, not far from his weapons rooms, lavishly outfitted in gold leaf. We saw the lord's office as well, with autographed pictures from the King of England and Pope St. Pius X, and in the next room, photographs of Ferdinand and his wife behind glass in various stages of their lives, and their death masks and, in a small box, the bullet that had started the war. Somebody near me joked that the assassin was probably just an early member of Greenpeace.

We went through a sitting room with huge bear rugs, poked our heads into a "harem room"—a sinister-feeling place with a low ceiling and decorated in wine red—the halls of which once witnessed the other sport

of lords. Downstairs we went through living quarters—
all as sumptuously decorated as the weapons rooms,
only here there were chandeliers of sparkling Bohemian
and Polish glass, and large, dramatic paintings of the
Habsburgs. Our guide pointed out one such painting of
a Habsburg couple with nearly identical hangdog ex-
pressions who had been thought of, during their time,
as "the ugliest couple in all of Europe." That they certainly were.

At the end of one hallway filled with Ferdinand's
deer, squirrel and bear conquests, there was a bathroom
which was, for the age, apparently quite advanced,
with hot running water for the sink and bath. I walked
in to glance around. Over the bathtub there was a
drawing, made by some "anonymous artist," the guide
later told me, of a woman standing in a large rowboat.
Behind her, the moon shone on the water and gave an
angelic glow to the smooth skin of her shoulders. Below her, in the boat, a man was kneeling, looking up
into her eyes, his hands extended toward her, trying to
embrace her. Her hands touched his, lightly, as if at the
moment of invitation, or rejection. The eerie, romantic
rendering seemed to me connected, at that moment in
my tour, to the strange forces that set some men to violence.

The dark hallways, the chandeliers, the paintings,
the weapons, the severed mounted heads, and the memory of the personages who still haunted that castle com-
bined to make me feel very low indeed. I was grateful
when we left and started our walk down the path
through the forest, perhaps a quarter mile to the bus.
The wind rustled through the leaves and through wild
grass. The trees were tall above me. The hill was of

moderate grade and my legs felt good making the descent and I could smell the forest and the earth there. My spirit lifted.

En route, I met a couple from Texas who were part of my tour group. Judy Rollins was a plump, smiling woman who seemed glad to have another American to talk to, but when her husband Kip spoke she kept an odd, critical eye on him. We talked about the strange juxtaposition of the Konopiště chapel and the weapons collection, and Judy and Kip told me about countries they had just been through (it was business for Kip as well as travel—he worked for an oil company): Bulgaria, Poland, France, Germany. In France, Kip told me, someone had picked his pocket. I said I'd met somebody that'd happened to back at St. Vitus' Cathedral. As our conversation progressed, Kip and Judy seemed to talk primarily about the *economic* state of the countries they'd visited. Buildings were described as run-down or well-kept, food was lousy or fair enough, and there was a constant, detailed listing of how much things had cost them. It dawned on me that they had taken in very little else about the places they had been to. Kip struck me as a man who felt little sensitivity toward others and had the capacity to become an ass if he needed to. His wife, pleasantly disguising her dominance over him, worked to smooth over his harsher sentences. I decided they were a strange couple, and that it would be nice to be on my own, but I could not muster the resolve to move away from them once we started talking.

At the bottom of the hill our tour guide said "Everyone to bus," and I was annoyed when I heard Kip, to his wife, imitate the guide's accent. I said, "I *like* the accent." Kip nodded agreeably and didn't get my meaning, and I had the thought that this was not a fellow you would want to have teach manners to your children.

We boarded the bus and our American military expert was busy telling some Italians, "Did you know that, after the Czechs killed Heydrich, Adolf Hitler had a whole town *razed* to the ground?" Mr. Crew-cut seemed to like the exactness and terror of the word *razed*, and he emphasized it with all of the force of his dark eyes, and the Italians, trying to appear properly wide-eyed and impressed by his story, clearly did not understand what he was saying at all. He talked on, oblivious, until finally they turned back to their seats and spoke some Italian gently to one another, and Crew-cut sat, staring forward, mulling over the gravity of his last few statements. Judy leaned forward from where she was sitting with Kip in the back and said, "Joe, would you please join us for lunch at Karlštejn?" I said of course I would and thanked her and when I turned back, I saw that Crew-cut, now that he realized I was an American, was looking at me with great consideration. I stared away from him and out the window forcefully, thinking that my country here was sorely represented.

And then we drove, and I watched ribbons of sunlight through trees and stretches of the golden fields on top of the hills, thankful that our host was telling us about the history of Karlštejn, the country castle of Charles IV, and I was relieved of any conversations. I slept a bit. When I woke we were pulling into a stop over the magnificent Vltava valley, a green, open expanse with the river winding lazily through, and a large health and recreation spa decorating its shores. As I looked down, a kayak race was going on on the river

far below, a rapid circle of small, colorful darts round-
ing a pylon. I descended the bus stairs with the others
for a few minutes, found a ledge with a good vantage
point, and pointed my Pentax and snapped away.

At Karlštejn, our host told us we had about a
twenty-five minute walk up the mountain to the place
where we would have lunch before entering the castle.
Or, she said, there were taxis you could take. Despite
my aching leg, I was happy for the chance at exercise.
Kip and Judy, along with some French tourists, opted
to take a taxi to the top ("Seven-hundred crowns for
five people," I overheard the taxi driver tell them now).
I walked alone for a while, looking up at the great
tower of the castle where once, according to tourist literature, King Charles had kept two thorns from Jesus'
crown, part of the sponge offered to Him on the Cross,
and a tooth from John the Baptist, among other religious relics. Soon I struck up a conversation with the
Irish woman who had found the weapons at Konopiště
"lovely" and the friend she was touring with. I realized
that they both used the adjective with most things, including the castle above us now, so it was benign, and
they were attractive women and animated and intelligent, and I started to hope that the taxi might take a
wrong turn so that I could sit with them at lunch. Un-
expectedly, some old acquaintances of theirs walked
out of a shop before us and the women stopped to chat,
and I said my hellos and told my new friends I would
see them above. I kept walking.
Just below Karlštejn, with the castle looming over
you, there is a small, tourist square with a simulated
Tyrolean restaurant, some gift shops, and a dungeon-
like bathroom where an old woman charges you four

crowns to get in and reminds you to take paper. In the center of this square, Kip and Judy were waiting for me, quite disturbed. Their taxi driver had demanded his seven-hundred crown fee even though four instead of five people had decided to ride in the car, and Kip had paid it, expecting the French couple to split it afterward with him. But the French couple had not understood the transaction and had objected to the price after the driver had gone, thinking Kip was cheating them, and something akin to a French-American skirmish had happened here, in the tourist square, while I was peacefully walking up from below. Though Kip was flustered, and talking quickly, my impression was that things had not come to blows—but it had been close. While Kip and Judy and I were considering the difficulties of debating financial terms in French, German, and English, Mr. Crew-cut spotted us from across the square and, without his eyes wavering from us once, came over.

"This is really something," he said. "I love this goddamned country. These poor Czechs. Did you know that after they killed that Nazi leader Heydrich, Hitler had this little town, Lidice, razed to the ground?"

I told him I'd heard the story.

"And Hitler ordered all the men just plain lined up and shot? And then these poor Czech people have to deal with these goddamned Commies." He shifted his weight a little, and screwed up his face into a practiced, cunning expression. "When I was stationed in Germany, we used to yell "Hey Ivan!" over the lines and these dumb Red bastards would just look at us. I never thought I'd be coming over here as a tourist. I thought I'd be wearing my little green uniform."

Kip and Judy Rollins engaged the man in conversation, and I was happy then to have them beside me. Somehow the conversation steered around to President Clinton.

"You don't think *he'd* have a major problem if he asked soldiers to go into battle?" Crew-cut said. "The guy's just a draft-dodging peacenik."

"Could be he did it as an act of conscience," I said, wanting suddenly and stupidly to offer an argument.

"Hell, *conscience*," Crew-cut said, snorting and eyeing me suspiciously. "He just didn't want to get into a little green *uni*form."

The tour guide had lost somebody now, and she was frantically searching for them, and people were filing into the Tyrolean restaurant for lunch. I looked up at the castle with longing. Right then, I couldn't wait to get up there, and get the tour over with, and get back to Mira's flat in the city.

Josef on skis. Zugspitze, Germany, 1954.

CHAPTER EIGHT

THE SAINT, THE PRIEST, AND THE CLOCK

In the year 1234 the Bohemian princess Agnes, sister of King Wenceslas I, founded her "convent for the Poor" in medieval Prague. From this act a legend grew that her canonization would mark the beginning of a miracle in her land.

She was elevated to sainthood seven hundred and fifty-five years later as, in the streets of her city, Czech citizens began to feel the stirrings of freedom in the air. Demonstrations during that November of 1989 had been going on since the previous fall, when Václav Havel was re-imprisoned (he had been serving sentences in jail, and under house arrest, for twelve years) after showing up at a memorial in Wenceslas Square for Jan Palach. That memorial service, on the spot where Palach sacrificed himself, had ended in police beatings. All through the year since, when Mira went onto the streets, she had felt the increased tension between citizens and police: it seemed as if, at any provocation, the beatings would begin.

Now, on the seventeenth of November, Mira was at the Tessla factory, bent over a set of blueprints at her drafting table. It was late afternoon, and she heard a commotion in the hallway. She opened the office door to see Anna Svojsikova, from the research department, saying to a group of wide-eyed co-workers: "It's the students. They are marching from Vyšehrad. There are thousands of them."

Fifteen thousand students and their compatriots were marching at that moment toward Wenceslas Square, hoping to reach a monument to Jan Opletal, a medical student shot during the Nazi oppression fifty years before. The Communists had forbidden the march, knowing that it was a disguised protest against them, and that the Wenceslas Square area, so rich in nationalist symbols, had often been a tinderbox of trouble. But the students were marching anyway, and their group was growing in number. Prague workers had left their jobs and joined them: as the demonstration turned and walked downriver, along Rasinovo, taxi drivers sped by, honking their horns in support; trams and buses stopped and let their passengers off to be a part of the demonstration.

My cousin Maruška Kublová, a student at Charles University, was in the procession that day. And Mira left the Tessla factory and joined them too: it was like entering a river of humanity. A father near her walked with a boy on his shoulders, and the boy clutched a Czech flag. A teen-aged girl walked beside Mira, her straight blond hair blowing, her round glasses catching the late light of the sky as she looked up at the buildings; above, high in the windows, people were shouting their encouragement. The teen-aged girl looked at Mira, and said: "They have big banners up front saying *We Don't Want Violence*. We're just going to show them that we're not afraid anymore." Mira could see some signs ahead dancing as students thrust them into the air. And now a chant started: "Wenceslas Square and then home!" Fists were in the air, pounding to the rhythm of the chant. Mira threw her fists up, too, and the blond girl looked over, clapping, saying the words happily.

The procession was, suddenly, fifty-five thousand strong. It went past the National Theatre, where actors and staff were at the windows, applauding. Looking at the graceful building on the Vltava, Mira thought of her mother, and then of her brother in prison. She remembered the Soviet tanks rolling through this city so long ago, crushing the Prague Spring. Most of these students could hardly have been born then, and yet they marched as if they felt every moment of the last forty years in their bones.

The demonstration turned onto Národní Avenue. It slowed and stopped, met ahead by a wall of police. The plexiglass-protected officers and the demonstrators drew to within three meters of one another. The Communist police shifted uneasily; the demonstrators held hands and sang *We Shall Overcome* and the national anthem, *Where Is My Home*. They sang a favorite song of President Masaryk's that Mira remembered from childhood, called *Oh my Son, my Son*. As Mira sang, she looked around her and everyone was singing, defiantly: many, like her, had tears in their eyes.

Students tossed flowers at the troops and put flowers in police rifles and lit candles on the ground. They held up alarm clocks and told the Communists that it was time for their regime to go. They closed their eyes and sang their songs. Quietly, from behind them, another force of police blocked off the demonstrators' route of escape. The Communists began moving forward.

Joined by an elite military force called the Červené Barety (Red Berets), the police swung their truncheons at the demonstrators. Under the quick rain of violence, the demonstrators tried to run. But they were caught and held and beaten mercilessly, and when they fell to the ground, the police kicked them with their boots. Students and elderly, parents and children, all were hit: some six hundred were injured.

In the front lines of the students, Maruška was beaten badly. Then Mira was shoved and fell. She rolled on the stones, a madness of legs and screams and blood around her, and thought *Surely I am finished now*. But student hands reached for her, and picked her up.

Later it would be discovered that undercover police, acting as protesters, had helped lead the demonstrators into the ambush, perhaps as part of a conspiracy to bring down the hard-line government and replace it with a leadership more in tune with Gorbachev. Whatever the truth, forces had suddenly been unleashed in Czechoslovakia which no Communist power or deception could hold in line.

Though official news reports tried to claim that it had been the students who created the violence, pictures of the beatings, distributed throughout the country, soon gave this familiar Communist story the lie. In shop windows in Prague, televisions with VCRs were set up to play underground videotapes of the November 17 police action. In front of theatres and art galleries, a collage of photographs of the beatings ran on screens continuously for gathered crowds. On the corner of Mikulandská and Národní, students placed hundreds of votive candles where blood still stained the ground.

An uneasy time followed: Mira told Maruška and her friends to use the apartment to hide from the police whenever they needed. For eight days following the November 17 demonstration, three hundred and fifty thousand people packed into Wenceslas Square, listening to dissident speeches and singing *We Shall Overcome*. In the Little Quarter of Prague, on the garden wall of the Grand Priory of the Knights of Malta, students scribbled the lyrics of John Lennon's *Imagine* near a colorful likeness of the rock star that had been there since his death. Václav Havel, out of prison now, gathered leading dissidents and workers and intellectuals and formed "Civic Forum," an umbrella organization for the various protest movements in the country, to provide a unified front in negotiations with the Communist regime. For its part, the Communist government was pressed into the stunning conclusion that, in order to maintain control of Czechoslovakia, it would have to kill on a mass scale: some in the Central Committee in fact advocated what they called a "Tiananmen Square" solution.

In the metro, where Mira traveled everyday, the students were filling the walls with words. *Remember the imprisoned as if you were imprisoned with them*, one graffiti message said. Next to it was a poster that read: *Havel didn't keep quiet when we were frightened to speak out. Now it's our turn.*

A few days after the beatings on Národní Avenue,

Mira stood with three-quarters of a million people in Letná stadium, watching the distant figures of Alexander Dubček (sixty-eight years old now and the enduring symbol of the 1968 Spring), and Václav Havel as they specified the demands of Civic Forum: an abolition of the constitutional guarantee of a leading role for the Communists in Czechoslovak government, personnel changes in leadership, and free elections. Their voices echoed over the crowd, and the applause for them grew around Mira like wind.

The famous dissident priest, Václav Malý, came on stage and introduced two StB agents, who apologized to the crowd for their long role in the oppression. As they spoke, Mira felt the mood around her changing, saw angry eyes trained on the nervous two figures on stage. The speakers finished their apology, and there was a hush of anger in that place, a flood of memories; of torture, of constant night fear: always there was the chance that the StB might come at four in the morning, beating on the door, taking a family member away forever. Here were two of the men responsible. As the crowd grew more restive, the priest stepped forward, and bowed his head.

Our Father, he said.

Who art in heaven, the vast audience said. Mira bowed her head and spoke the words. The sound of all of those voices in unison was enormous. She was in a sea of prayer.

In December, when CF leaders called for a nationwide strike, gaining the favor even of the Communists' traditional and essential constituency—the industrial workers—the power of the regime was broken. By the end of the month, the Communist government had fallen to this nonviolent "Velvet Revolution."

"They had arms," Havel would say later, when he had become president. "We had the truth."

So on a bright May morning in 1993 I took a tram to Holesovice street, to the St. Anton church, where Father Václav Malý was just finishing mass. Afterward, when the priest had shed his vestments in a back room to reveal a striped sport shirt and casual pants, we walked together to the sidewalk where life in the Prague 7 Quarter moved at a high pace. Passers-by greeted their priest and made requests and statements that he answered enthusiastically and quickly: the tram running through the street next to us clanged by so loudly that sometimes we could not hear one another. Dogs barked in the distance and birds called from the rooftops above. Occasionally a car whizzed by, its tires thundering on the stones. To me, the vibrant area seemed an appropriate place to be interviewing the priest of the Velvet Revolution.

Malý had consistently defied the Communist state during his adult life, and was picked up and interrogated some two hundred and fifty times by the StB. They had beaten him, harassed and followed him, and imprisoned him with Václav Havel when, in 1979, he was charged with subversion for his membership in "the committee for the defense of unjustly persecuted citizens." His license to work officially as a priest had been canceled and so, when he was released from prison, he tried to work first in a hospital, and then washing windows. Both requests were denied. Finally, he was given a job stoking coal in several hotels for four years, and then dug ditches in the Soviet-constructed subway under Prague for another four. With Havel, he became one of the founders of Civic Forum, and a spokesman for the liberation of his nation. It would come as no surprise to me when, in December of 1996, midway through this writing, I would learn that Pope John Paul II had elevated Father Malý's position to that of Bishop.

On this May morning, speaking in his slightly broken, energetic English, the forty-three year-old priest told me that he was not bitter about his long persecution at the hands of the Communists.

"(The Communist period) was good for me," Malý said, "because I came into contact with usual workers. It was very important for me to have to express my faith in a civic way. Obviously, it wasn't a nice time. But one must see positive things from that period. Personally, it helped me . . . the Communists helped me deepen my faith."

The Communist era had offered his countrymen the lesson of "knowing personal conviction through sacrifice," he said, and the opportunity to "win certain spiritual values." It deepened for all of them the meaning of their current freedom. Freedom, according to Malý, didn't mean "simply to do what one wants, but to accept personal limitations: then one is really free." One must find a place inside, he seemed to suggest, where oppressive forces, whatever they may be, are not allowed entrance into the soul—and thus one gains true personal freedom.

An older woman came up to us, asking Malý some questions in rapid Czech. He answered her quickly but thoroughly, apparently, dispatching her down the street. He smiled at me, and nodded for me to continue.

I asked him for his feelings about the younger generation that had engined the revolution. It was a subject, I realized, that consumed him. He told me about the challenges for Czech youth: they had grown up in an atmosphere of forced silence, and now needed a grounding in the truth from their leaders.

"The freedom came so fast, so suddenly," he said, "that people weren't ready for it. For forty years one kept silent about certain values and now this generation is searching, and there is a danger of consumerism filling that space. Under Communism, much was clear: (it) offered an empty ideology and an alternative spiritual program, and one could make decisions accordingly. But now there are many other offers and this generation is a little confused. It wants to grasp certain values at once without the benefit of personal labor.

"Economically," he said, "our problems will be solved very soon. But it will take two generations to (recover) spiritually because people have lost a spiritual sense for certain values—for example, *humility, forgiveness, hope, communication*. The Communists denied these values. They didn't even mention them. They emphasized only the 'class struggle' and built a mutual mistrust into the thinking of people. The first very important matter is for us to start to trust one another again."

In our intense discussion about consumerism, ("Compete, yes, *good*," Malý told me, "but not at the *expense* of others,") Malý seemed determined that I understand his distinction between "individuality" and "individualism." *Individuality*, he said, was essential to all people: one must have self-respect and not be afraid to stand up for one's values, to be a "ward of one's own dignity." *Individualism*, on the other hand, was the selfish process through which, in the stampede for profit and success, one thought nothing of trampling over the weak. It was the influx of consumerism and profit at any price into the values of his nation that was the greatest danger to the youth of the Czech Republic. He quizzed me to make sure I'd understood him fully.

"It is a problem of all Western democracies," he said, satisfied that I had it down properly. "Everything is oriented now in the technological dimension. And this misses a humanism, a humanistic thinking, a humanistic education, and I would say that this is dangerous."

Here, at the center of his parish, as Father Malý spoke, I imagined him in prison, imagined him beaten— this good man of conscience. I imagined him bowing his head in Letna stadium, bringing faith into a moment that promised violence. I asked him about it, and he smiled at the memory.

"I wanted to attract attention to the fact that without God's blessing our actions wouldn't be possible . . . that the revolution was not only done through Havel and his friends but that it was above all a matter of heaven," he told me. "It was a very special feeling, a very strange feeling, because of the risk involved that I would be rejected. That it was successful wasn't my merit but the merit of God."

He had seen his place in the revolution as a peaceful link between revolutionary and Communist forces, and once this connection had been solidly established he effectively ended his political activity. "It doesn't mean I am not interested in politics—on the contrary—" he said, "but I reject further involvement in the structures of power."

I asked him now: what is your definition of courage?

He laughed a little. Then he thought and said: "Above all to live a one-faced life. To have something *in*side, and reflect this *out*side. And not only to reflect the truth in the heart but to live according to the truth."

We had talked for thirty-five minutes, and Father Malý was late for his next appointment. When he left me, running up the street with a wind-jacket slung over his shoulder, turning back once to wave, I felt I had gone through a transformation. It was not an uncommon sensation for me in Bohemia: to feel suddenly and solidly fused to humanity through the courage of those who had fought for it, through individuals like this animated, indefatigable priest.

The concrete eastern wall of Pankrác prison is decaying and soiled, and when you stand before it there is a small water tower to your right. The water tower leads to another wall topped with barbed wire. On the overcast day that I visited the prison with Mira the barbed wire was a silhouette against the flat white sky.

There is a gate in the middle of the eastern wall with a corrugated steel door and two ugly lamps above. Running by the wall is a long, gray parking strip. Mira told me about how my grandmother had walked here, up and down, praying for her son. She told me that Barbora could hear the workers with their hammers inside building scaffolding for the executions.

We walked together around the prison grounds then, not saying very much. There was grief and silence inside me, for my grandmother and my father, and for all the people who had been here. How many had died here, how many had been tortured? How many lives wasted for the philosophies of the mad? The buildings were old and falling into disrepair at every point: by the courtroom with its statue of justice at the side of the

entrance, and by the red brick and garish blue door entrance to the "health facilities," where once Václav
Havel must have gone when he had nearly died of
pneumonia and world opinion had demanded that he
be saved.

Rising over the prison roofs I could see the clock
tower, jutting up, painted red. I stopped and watched
it, imagining a terrifying silence as the clock-hands
reached the hour, and horror within the prison: those
on death row suddenly realizing, *no bells*. What did
they think of then? How did they prepare themselves? I
watched the hands of the clock in that odd, white day.

The clock tower at Pankrác prison.

CHAPTER NINE

SHADOWS

Eleven days into my journey, Mira and I stood before the grave of my grandmother in Žebrak. The Communists, to humiliate my family, had made it difficult for Mira to have Barbora buried beside my grandfather in Radnice. Mira had written my father in the United States and asked, What should I do? And my father, to ease things for Mira at that terrible time, said It is fine if she is in Žebrak. I believe so, too, and that the spirits of my grandmother and grandfather must, somewhere, be together.

The cemetery was peaceful and sunny and you could see, beyond, the hills surrounding the town. Above us, in the trees and telephone lines, were the songs of the afternoon spring birds. Mira wept and touched the stone and crossed herself and said to her mother, "He is here now." I touched the stone also, and thought about my time with this kindly and precocious woman in the woods of Massachusetts, collecting acorns. I had been four. I could remember the pine-needled floor and the smell of the forest, and how my grandmother had bent over, gathering the brown acorns, and held them up in her hand for me to see. She had told me about the people we would make out of them. I reached down to gather them with her and somehow, as she'd spoken Czech to me, I had understood everything she'd said. We brought the acorns indoors and painted faces together on them beneath their "hats." In my imagination, I remembered now, each of them had acquired a distinctive personality.

I saw my grandmother as a young actress, smiling and laughing, dancing with my grandfather somewhere in a hall in this village, her hands on his broad shoulders. Then all of those years later, holding photographs by the edges—watching images of her son curl and darken to ash. Being given his bloody coat by the StB, touching it to her face when they had left the apartment.

I remembered now my grandmother's death, just a few years after her only visit to the United States: I'd come in from being outside with friends that day, and my mother had made me quiet and serious with a look of her eyes.

"What's wrong?" I'd said.

"Daddy's mother died," my mother said.

I'd gone into the living room. There, my father sat in an armchair, weeping. I had never seen him cry before.

We put flowers by the grave and watered them, and then walked through the paths of the cemetery, Mira pointing out the burial sites of relatives and friends. Generations of my family were here. I passed by a grave reading 'Josef Hurka'—a disconcerting feeling, looking at my name on a gravestone, and learned from Mira that this was a cousin of ours who, on the night before his own wedding, had given my father a ride on motorcycle to the last safehouse my father had stayed in, in Kladruby. I thanked this cousin, silently, and we went on our way.

The following morning, on a train to Radnice, I watched the Bohemian countryside go by: fields of green and gold, and small, rural, agricultural areas. The train car ran alone on an electrical track, and Mira told me that, when she and my father were children, the train had been quite different, wooden, and not this fiberglass and plastic affair we were in.

We sat quietly for a time, listening to the wheels clack along peacefully. I wondered why, despite all he'd been through here, my father had not returned to his homeland since the revolution. I thought of Father Malý saying two generations needed to go by for the country to recover spiritually, and I remembered the face of Mr. Pok on the plane and his warning that my father not return. Four years later I would ask my father directly about it. He quietly repeated things I'd heard before: he was angry about the treatment former friends had given Mira and my grandmother, and wondered if he could keep his temper if he ran into them (I doubted it). And he told me of his anger that a number of former Communist bosses now lived as wealthy capitalists in the country they had destroyed. The Czech government, he said, ought to grab such people by their throats and administer justice to them, and the Communist Party needed to be banned altogether from the

Czech Republic. "To some, these things don't matter as much," he told me, "but I am one of those who is greatly bothered by them."

All of this made sense, but I had the feeling that there was something deeper at work, and I pursued him on it.

"Look," he said emphatically, "all of us, everyone involved during that time—the Communists, me, everyone involved in the fight—all of us must die for the country to be what it once was." The phrase stunned me at first, and then its meaning slowly took root in me: my father felt he was part of something the country needed to be rid of. He had come to this on principle, and the only reason he would shake from it and return would be to briefly see his mother and father. Riding across Bohemia on this day in 1993 I think I somehow already understood this in my bones. The Czech Republic certainly was not the same country my father and Mira had lived in as children.

We passed over a deep gorge on a high bridge, and then wound through a forest. Then, ahead in a small valley, there was a sketch of white and pastel buildings, and we went into a turn behind some greenery. We came up to a station on a slight hill and the train slowed and stopped and we descended from the stairs. The train station was a simple, modest place, and a little farther down the tracks there were silos, and on the station wall there was a sign that read: *Radnice*.

Mira and my father's hometown had the appearance I'd come to expect of these small Bohemian villages—buildings close together, streets and sidewalks all intricate stone. As we walked downhill from the station, I could not help seeing that the town was more worn-out than I'd expected from pictures: the houses, which had once been impregnated with bold color, now were gray, and many of the sidewalks were broken and dusty. There had been a felling of trees and an installation of ugly streetlights in the town square when the Communist town government, some years before, had adopted the "progressive" slogan that it was "not possible to live like in the old days." It looked like a community that had once been affluent but had, at some critical point, during some calamity, lost its source of income, its lifeblood.

But there were also signs of hope: in the town square, many of the old shops were being renovated. And there rising above the square was the Radnice church. I recognized it from the old pictures that Mira had. It stood proudly, a red and burnished color and with a black clock beneath its curving Bohemian steeple. It was Zdeněk Blecha, my father's childhood friend, who in older age had rebuilt the clock when it finally needed fixing. He had since passed away, but we would stay with his family tonight, just a few blocks from here.

Beyond the church were the hills: Kalvárie, where I could see a small chapel among the trees, and to the left Hůrka, which in the ancient Czech language meant "guard." Across the valley was Florian, where my father had left dynamite for the Resistance. I glanced at Mira. She walked slowly, but I thought of her here, fifty-five years before, bright eyes and skipping with friends as they all got off the train from school. And I was moving back into a place of my own as well: some chord of childhood that I was familiar with, like the chord of a guitar. There was a mystery here, waiting for me in this quiet valley.

We stepped down the hill; Mira seventy-one now, and just moments ago a young girl with all of life before her.

Not far from the center of Radnice, Hana Blechová lives in a graceful wooden building that reminds one of an American farmhouse in the Midwest. There is an iron gate that you must pass through, and a large garage where young Zdeněk (just a few years older than I) does his mechanical work, like his father and grandfather once did. There is an old Russian car in the yard and a number of roosters and a thin, rather slow collie named Jack that quickly accompanies you wherever you go. There is a small building in the yard that was, apparently, a tiny chapel for a previous owner.

The downstairs area of the house is occupied by Hana, and this is where we went and were greeted at the door by this feisty, warm woman. The Blechas were one of the few families that remained true to Mira and my grandmother during the Communist occupation; through those years, Hana made her living helping manage a collective farm. She has mischievous, humorous eyes and you feel, immediately, that she is your friend. Hana had prepared lunch for us: soup and pork chops and some sauerkraut which I deftly pushed aside. We were soon joined by Hana's granddaughter, Michal, and Zdeněk. Michal, thin and shy and blushing, apparently, at my presence, had just come home for lunch from school, which was just a few blocks down the road. Her mother, Vladka, was still at work there in the cafeteria, but would meet us later.

In the living room some time after, when Michal had gone back to classes, Hana repeated some funny stories to me that her husband had told her.

"After your father beat up Ada Vostrý," she said, "everyone was awful to Ada, because they saw they could be. Some of the boys tied him to a tree and peed on him from the upper branches."

We howled and hooted at this. When she'd gotten her laughter under control, Hana continued:

"—and once they took turns rolling Ada in a patch of poison ivy. He was miserable for weeks."

I said it seemed like Ada the bully had the "open season" on him coming. It was a fitting end to his legend.

Zdeněk took me that afternoon to see the places of our fathers. With Mira and Hana, we drove in Zdeněk's Volkswagen Golf through the town and up Kalvárie hill—in New Hampshire it would be called a small mountain. Up, up, we went, through a forest on a dirt road, the black trees and branches silhouettes against a fire of more distant green leaves and light. We emerged at a sloping field where the road ended and the white Volkswagen stopped next to a little cottage that overlooked the long grass and wildflowers. The field had apple trees planted on sections of it now, the only difference, Mira told me, from when children of her generation used to hike up here: the change had been made, she said, because if the Communists had not been convinced there was a functional use for the field, it would have been taken over for use by the State.

Above us, on the crest of the hill, Mira pointed to a spot where the Communists had constructed a foxhole: it was now growing over with weeds. I said: "That is good. The thing should grow over with weeds." Beyond it, she said, out of our sight, were more fields of the glowing řepka flower: it was a spot the locals called *Na Nebesích*, or "place in the sky."

Zdeněk, saying he would do a few errands and then meet us below, drove off in the VW and left us so that we could enjoy the walk down. As we descended again into the brilliantly-lit forest, Mira told me stories about her childhood here. Hana, a few steps ahead of us, collected flowers at the side of the road for me to press into a book and bring back to my father. We branched off from the road and went down a steep, rambling dirt path; soon we were on streets and among houses again. Crickets sawed in the bushes near an old pond, and the sun lit on the sidewalks, and here and there a shadow slanted from a jutting stone.

On Švehlova street we came up to number 145. This was where my father and Mira had grown up, where my grandfather once set up his leather shop, and where my grandmother continued to live until she and Mira were forced to sell the home during the early years of Communist rule. Mira told me my father would be disappointed in how it looked; no longer a bright lime-green, the mortar walls were now gray and beaten by age. When you face the building, it seems narrow, as most of these houses do (it is their depth that gives them their living space). The five windows that looked onto the street were in fine shape, but a small garbage can sat conspicuously at the side of the residence and the carefully-laid stone sidewalk that was once in front of it had been replaced by slabs of concrete. Pale and worn, the old house seemed to tell me the story of my family: of peace, and war, separation and endurance.

We picked up Michal after school and the Volkswagen zipped efficiently into the countryside; we drove into the Brdy mountains, and followed the

Berounka river near Liblin and Zvíkovec. Zdeněk motored the Golf a few miles up a long country road and into what looked like a forest driveway, dirt, bumpy, steep. The drive finally leveled off and where we parked the forest had ended and directly to our left was a dramatic field of řepka. I got out of the car, in awe of its stunning brightness, acres and acres of it, and the way it calmly rustled with wind. I looked carefully. For a moment I felt like the ghost soldiers were there, a legion of them: I sensed that perhaps they were trying to tell me something. The wind picked up and the brilliant field hissed beneath the sun.

We walked a twisting path through wood and brush to our right. It came to its end on rock, and I looked out and realized that I was standing on a craggy cliff, and hundreds of feet below was the Berounka, a silver sluice beneath the sky. Our fathers had canoed here often, Zdeněk told me. I could see a bridge and a few sets of gentle rapids. To the right, a road with a few tiny houses meandered off and found, eventually, a small village in the distance. In the hills farther up to the left, there were the ruins of an ancient castle, gazing over the valley.

I was still thinking of the ghosts, but I saw no sign of them as we walked by the field again, to the Golf.

At the Radnice cemetery that evening, standing at my grandfather's gravestone, Mira was sad, but not with the same desperation shown at the grave of her mother. Time had taken away some of the sorrow at the circumstances of my grandfather's death, and she was proud of her father, and glad that he was here, in this peaceful place.

I said hello to my grandfather: It's nice to finally

meet you. I was proud of him, too, proud that, even in death, he had been a community leader: the procession of his funeral through the streets of Radnice in 1944 had been a quiet anti-Nazi demonstration. In pictures Mira had shown me, my grandmother watched the burial as if she could not believe it was happening, and Mira behind her was full of controlled emotion. My father held his mother in one photograph, comforting her, and in another he leaned forward to the casket, and you could see only the top of his head and his shoulders. I do not think my father was kissing the casket or performing any religious rite, for he is not a religious man. But I think, in his own way, he was getting close to his father to say goodbye.

My father chose the spot in the graveyard. A chapel of St. Rosalia was close to us, just a few steps up the hill, and there were graves nearby dating back to the sixteen-hundreds. From my grandfather's spot you could see over parts of Radnice, and to the south were the hills where the children once had so much fun growing up, skiing and playing in caves. I believe my grandfather lives with them in spirit, in that time, and he speaks to me sometimes now from that happier age. My father chose a good place for him.

Late that night, in the comfortable bedroom Hana had given me, I wrote. The moths danced quietly in and out of the open windows, and the words that came made sketches, scenes from the past in my notebook:

Someone once asked Josef, when he was a boy, what he would like to be when he grew up.

He saluted.

This is his story:

Of Radnice, and the chatter of birds on the church

and telephone wires, of the muted sound of the church bell ringing the hour. The smells of flowers growing in the gardens throughout town, the sounds of cvrček (crickets) and rushing water beneath the bridge. When he is old enough he follows that small creek back with friends through one neighborhood to a pond where swans, in the spring, dip their heads into the dark, clear water to feed. All of his life, Josef will think of this place.

And of learning to ski: his uncle Jiří's strong hands beneath his arms, holding him up as he weaves on the curved wooden boards. Cold air on his face and his sister's laughter behind him, snow whistling and singing under him. And elementary school: walking there in the mornings with Mira and his parents, watching the way the early light shimmers on the sidewalks.

He'll see his father's precise hands as they hold a straightedge over sheets of leather for shoe and briefcase stock, the pieces coming out neat and stacked in an orderly fashion on the table. His father always talks to him and tells him stories as he works. Afterwards, there is soccer with friends, or climbing to the top of Kalvárie, where you walk through the golden fields and it is like walking through magic. And then coming home run-down, fresh-air tired for dinner and a bath and bed, and sleeping with the smell of the pond coming though the windows.

Life is not without trouble, though, for young Josef.

At the age of seven, he is given the duty, as many of the town boys are, of guarding the grave of Christ in the Radnice church. Depending on who you get to do the duty with, this vigil can be a blessing or a curse.

It is a curse with the Tereba brothers, Petr and Vladimír, for instance. They are older than Josef and

179

sometimes push him around when the priest is not watching. One Saturday, they laugh derisively about a boy Josef knows and likes.

You shouldn't talk that way, Josef tells them.

Yeah, Says who? the brothers mock him.

I say, Josef tells them, with a new and great fear fluttering in his chest.

You say, the brothers laugh.

Outside, on the lawn beside the church that is under the trees, Josef tries to leave quickly when duty is over, but the Tereba brothers catch him. They roll him onto the ground. They rip the shirt his mother has sewn for him, and they kick him. Josef sees trees, sky, in a blinding rush, and wishes he were stronger. A foot hits him in midsection, a terrible, sickening strike that makes him want to retch across the grass. Then the boys are running: Josef sees their figures move away from him and swiftly down the road. After they are gone it is a moment before he can raise himself. He walks carefully, his body shaking with anger and humiliation. When he gets home, he does not want to tell his mother, does not want his father to see him this way, would do anything for his father not to see him this way. But his father holds him gently and says "Pepa, you tell us who did this to you, they had to be big boys." And he does and looks up through fierce tears and there is nothing gentle in his mother's stare when she hears the name.

She storms out the front door. Josef never knows what happens at the Tereba household, but the brothers do not bother him again.

Many years later he wakes up in a safehouse in western Bohemia. The bedroom he has been given is dark and he listens to what disturbed him: the distant, frantic barking of dogs. He sits up and reaches for his pistol in the drawer beside him with his left hand; his right arm still hardly has any mobility, and aches so much that he has great difficulty sleeping these days. He puts a clip in his right hand. Slowly he manages to put it into the FN. He takes two other clips from the drawer and puts them in his shirt pocket.

Strangely, it was Radnice he was dreaming of just before the barking woke him, but he cannot remember what he saw there. He slides out of bed and clumsily pulls on pants. He walks down the stairs and goes outdoors, huddling near a pillar of the old structure. The pillar is protected by a few bushes, and he looks in the direction of the sound. It is coming from the road. Below him is a group of cherry trees and a shed, the moon making its roof nearly pale. By the shed is the worn path where he and General Seydl walked earlier this evening. The cicadas are singing in the fields. He leans out a little and looks up at the house. The old couple has not turned on any lights. He turns and glances at the path winding around the old farmhouse and out of his sight. It's anybody's guess whether the StB will circle around to get him: that would be the logical way. In any case, the old couple will suffer awfully when they are arrested, and the thought of it makes Josef swim in despair.

There are more dogs barking on the road now—a chain of them up and down at least a mile. Josef thinks of Cheb, of how Pišta looked in that moment after the gunfire, and of his own run to Prague. It seems, somehow, that he has been fighting forever.

Now, suddenly, the dogs have stopped. Have the StB, furious at the noise, killed them? He strains his eyes at the field and the shed. Nothing is there but the farm and the cicadas and the night.

And yet they are here. They have hunted him for two months and this is the end of it. He must remember, in his excitement, that when the firing starts he'll have only the seven bullets. He may not be able to get another clip into the pistol fast enough. He'd better take five shots and have two in case. Then without thinking he must put the gun into his mouth and fire.

And then in the shadows of the cherry trees below he sees a man.

It is a quick movement from one dark patch to another, but it was certainly a man holding a Sten: Josef saw where the strap off the man's shoulder met the straightness of the barrel, saw the profile of the man's head, and now he sees another man, crouching outside the shed in the high grass. They'll be coming from behind him, too. They'll want him alive so that they can kill him slowly while he tells them everything he knows about his skupina. *Well I won't be telling you anything, comrades.*

So enough of that now. There are these two before you and you can kill them. And then you can turn and maybe shoot one as he comes in from behind. Then you should probably get on with the business. But God forbid the left arm is shaking. Josef aims at that first black hulk of man but the left arm shakes uncontrollably. *Goddamnit,* he thinks, *not my nerves, not after I made it all this way.*

A dog barks in the distance again. The shadows below the cherry trees flicker, and Josef sees again the one with the rifle and strap, and it blows back and forth, back and forth. It is only a shadow and leaves.

The wind rustles over the farm. It bends the tall

sunflowers in the old woman's garden. Josef slumps against the pillar. He thinks angrily: now you have a nervous breakdown over a bunch of dogs and shadows. He steadies his breathing: you are a little hysteric, he tells himself. Be aware of it and let the pain in your arm clear your head a little. One thing at a time, Pepa, because you are not yourself, and you might have shot at two shadows and then killed yourself, all alone here, on this farm tonight.

After a time he goes upstairs again to the bedroom, but he cannot sleep for the sound of his heart beating in his ears.

*   *   *

In the morning, Mira and I took the bus from the center of the village. Hana stayed there watching us, waving, until she was a small figure in the early light; our bus worked up through the turning streets, the sun suddenly blinding through our windows. I shaded my eyes, saw sidewalks, gray walls, stove-pipe chimneys. Then there was a flash of green landscape, the grass dancing with morning wetness, and Radnice was gone.

Josef, around 1950.

CHAPTER TEN

LIBERATION

It was snowing in Deštná, in southern Bohemia, on the first of January, 1990. Mira was staying there for the holidays with Maruška Kublová and her large family at their farm in the country. In Prague, a government was being reborn.

At one o'clock that afternoon, the family gathered around the television to hear Václav Havel's first major speech as president:

My dear fellow citizens, he began,

For forty years you heard from my predecessors on this day different variations on the same theme: how our country flourished, how many million tons of steel we produced, how happy we all were, how we trusted our government, and what bright perspectives were unfolding in front of us.

I assume you did not propose me for this office so that I, too, would lie to you.

The new president outlined the desperate economic, educational, and ecological situations that the Communists had left Czechoslovakia in, and then told his countrymen to have hope, and to draw spiritually on the peaceful revolution they had just effected. There were strong reasons why the young and old could join together in such a dramatic revolt, he said:

. . . first of all, people are never just a product of the external world, but are also always able to relate themselves to something superior, however systematically the external world tries to kill that ability in them; second, the humanistic and democratic traditions . . . did after all slumber in the unconsciousness . . . and were inconspicuously passed from one generation to another so that each of us could discover them at the right time and transform them into deeds.

Reflecting Tomáš Masaryk's view that political activity must be grounded in morality, and Havel's own wish that Czechoslovakia might now become a beacon of "love, the power of the spirit and ideas," the new president expressed his vision for the future of his country:

Let us teach ourselves and others that politics can be not only the art of the possible . . . but . . . even . . . of the impossible, namely the art of improving ourselves and the world . . .

People, he said, *your government has returned to you!*

Mira and the family cried together with happiness. Later that afternoon they walked outdoors, talking and laughing, and when Mira looked up she could see a sky of infinite snow. On her mittened hand the snowflakes looked like small angels.

Nearing the end of my stay during this May of 1993, I walked one day with my aunt to meet Jana Pazlarová for some sightseeing in the city. Near Bethlehem Square Mira quietly stopped me and pointed to one building down a street of old, baroque structures. "I knew a woman who worked there cleaning, Joe," she told me. "It was where the Communists tortured many people. She finally went insane."

We walked in silence for a good while afterward, out of respect for those violated in that place and the terrible story of that woman.

Later, at Jana's apartment just off Vinohradská, the three of us looked at a picture of Václav Havel on the wall of Jana's sitting room. "He has the most wonderful *eyes*," Jana told me, recounting a meeting with the president. Over drinks and a delicious dinner of filet of beef and dumplings, or what the Czechs call Svíčková na smetaně, I watched the evening light fall on Laubova street below. It lit gracefully on a large rubber plant that Jana had near the window.

Jana asked me, with a twinkle in her eye, how I found the girls in the Czech Republic, and I told her that they were striking. Mira told Jana that one woman had given me her phone number on the metro. "Just like his father," Mira said.

"Your father was always a romantic," Jana said. "A poet. He liked very much to write things."

I knew this was true. I thought about books I had discovered as a boy in our garage in Massachusetts, tattered and forgotten but once, obviously, created with care—thick manuscripts with stories about love and war and fictional spy work, some written in Czech, some in German, others worked out in English when my father was trying to train himself in the language.

I had learned by this point not to bring up my father's Resistance activities, never knowing how much friends or family had been privy to it. But it was clear that Jana knew what my father had done.

"Why doesn't your father come back here?" she asked me, through Mira. "Does he still think there would be danger from the Communists?"

It wasn't an unreasonable question. I knew there were still Communists in the Czech Republic who probably hated my father. But I knew that that wasn't the reason he stayed away.

"It isn't really that," I said. "I think there are too many dark memories here."

Jana nodded at this seriously. "For all your father did, he should get a medal from President Havel."

I had a momentary image of my father, in his older age, approaching the president in some chandelier-lit room of the castle: generations of resistance meeting in a handshake. It brought sudden tears to my eyes.

"That would be good," I said. "I don't know if my father would accept it, but he sure deserves a medal."

I looked at Havel on the wall. I imagined, then, a scene I had not witnessed. Of that January evening in Vermont: my father walking across the family room, switching on the television, standing before that light. There was Havel on CNN, saying *your government has returned to you*, and pictures of candles being lit by children in Wenceslas Square. My father remembered a Christmas when he was a child, sixty years before: he was lighting candles with his mother, and she hummed an old, Bohemian tune to him. He could clearly remember that song. As commentators began discussing the liberation of his country, he turned off the television and stepped through the garage to the whiteness outside. Snow had just fallen and it sparkled on the birch trees, and through them my father watched the blue Taconic mountains and a bright winter moon.

At Mira's apartment the following evening I got ready to go to Wenceslas Square, for I was determined that, no matter how worn-out my leg was, I would see some of the night life in Prague before flying back to the United States. Mira made dinner, and on the Tessla we watched the Liverpool Symphony, just down the road at the Rudolfinum theatre by the river, preparing to give a performance of Smetana's *Má Vlast*. Most nights I would have stayed and watched with Mira, but tonight I was eager to get out on the town. I ate quickly, and stayed long enough to see Václav and Olga Havel arrive on the balcony and wave, briefly, to the audience. Then, as the first swirling notes of the symphony climbed with the bows of the violins, I was out the door, assuring Mira repeatedly that I would not be ambushed by any criminals.

Ten minutes later I came up at the Museum exit from the underground metro, the city, now at eight-thirty, looking distinctly unlike the one I'd known when I'd emerged here so many times before. Now there was no bright sunshine, but instead the neon lights and violet sky above. The storefronts were dark and the crowd on the sidewalks was younger, men and women dressed for dating. The women were made-up and laughing, their dresses flowing away from them as they walked the sidewalks in groups.

Bars were slowly filling with people, and movie theatres were midway through their first shows of the night. I put my head into one theatre where there was a famous American suspense thriller in progress, and, seeing the Czech subtitles, I thought momentarily about how much our two countries would mean to each other in the future, our pasts so inextricably linked.

At one club on Wenceslas square there was some furious rock music playing, the words of which I could not understand. It was quite dark and, beneath a glittering disco-ball, some teen-aged girls were dancing together, dressed to the nines. One of them looked at me, I felt, with disdain. I left, feeling I had grown too old for this or had somehow stepped onto the wrong planet.

It felt good and sane to get out of there, to be out on the Wenceslas Square I knew, the shops familiar, the air unrestricted. I walked down past the huge Bata shoe store and by the American hospitality center and then I was into the Old Town Square, a beautiful place at night. I looked up at the old clock, thinking about all the years people had watched time move on here. The steeples of Týn church rose up dramatically, their thin points in the night nearly unintelligible. It was quiet, with only a few tourists walking through, all of their eyes, like mine, turned up to the great church, and the ancient buildings and spires. Light from the old lamps fell across the cobblestones. The statue of Jan Hus was lit against the night, his cheekbones high and fierce. I thought of him burning in flames five hundred and seventy-eight years before, speaking to a God that his executioners could not see.

Suddenly, as I looked around, this ancient city Square seemed alive with spirits a half-millennium old, their bright streaks of torches burning as they gathered before Týn, calling for their martyr. The old church spoke to me with the great dignity of the ages; I had wondered, many times on this trip, how humankind could survive the extraordinary cruelty that had happened in so many places here, and whether humanity could overcome the drive for tribal war that seemed interwoven with each turn of history. The answer was Prague. It still stood, defiantly and gracefully, and humankind would march on.

I could write about that. And I could write about my father, eliminated from the history of his country: maybe the purpose of my journey was to write him back into that history. I decided now I would try.

I took a long last look at the spires, knowing that I would not be seeing them again for some time to come. Then I walked slowly back toward the Museum metro stop, glancing into various nightclubs along the way, but with little interest left for them. I descended into the green modern brightness of the subway and took the underground train back to the Flora stop. My naked fruit calendar girl looked sad for me tonight as I passed her, as if she knew that I would be leaving soon.

On my last full day, I went to Bertramka and got that scarf for Mira that she had liked so much. I would give it to her that evening. I wished I could give her more, for all that she had given me. Then I rode the metro to Wenceslas Square and put a flower in the Circle of Martyrs. I watched the signs and pictures of all those who had sacrificed for their country. I thought of my father and Pišta. I thought of Jan Palach, burning. Above me, St. Wenceslas raised his flag to the sun.

I went home to packing, wondering how the devil I would manage to get all of the things I had collected, maps, brochures, icons, gifts, notes and books, stuffed into my bags. That's what I tried to do: I tried to stuff it all. Mira watched, her face one of carefully-controlled amusement, and when I was frustrated enough she helped me with a lifetime of efficiency guiding her hands, and the deed was done in minutes.

Dr. Josef Macek.

CHAPTER ELEVEN

A PRAYER

On the bus to the airport the following morning, with Mira sitting beside me, I stood and held onto a hand-rail, staring out at the poorer parts of the city going by, and I thought about Havel's sanity, about freedom newly won and newly appreciated. I thought of the faces that had welcomed me, and all that I had learned here.

Mira was beside herself when we said goodbye at the airport. Farewells are difficult for her, representing as they do a kind of death. I hugged her, and looked at her eyes, and we said we would see each other again. I went through glass doors into customs. There, beyond her vision, I waited in a large lobby for my 12:20 plane. I passed through one other lobby, and then walked down stairs and outside with a group of travelers, heading for the Fokker that waited to take us to Copenhagen. There were some Aeroflot jets near us, the sickle and hammer still painted high on their tails. The wind blew in gusts and a few raindrops hit my face.

A number of umbrellas fought the gusts on a balcony above, and I thought Mira might be there. I waved in that direction. The stewardess nodded to me and I took a last glance around at the green surrounding the airfield, and ascended the steps. Sitting in the airplane, looking out the window—a tense oval of raindrops and the buildings beyond—I thought of a line I might say one day to my grandchildren, after describing my trip, that *This was how the Czech Republic was in 1993, when I flew from it back to my home in America.*

Then we were in the air, and below me, in that gray day, the Czech Republic disappeared quite rapidly.

During Christmas of 1992, at his home in Vermont, my father received a "declaration" from the Czech Supreme Military Court in Tábor. In this statement, which rescinded his conviction of 19 September, 1949, Lieutenant Josef Hůrka, of military unit 54-36, Hradec Králové, was exonerated for the following crimes:

1. Forbidden intelligence activity.
2. Spreading false rumors.
3. Removing himself from his military unit without permission.
4. Acting against customary regulations.
5. Acting against regulations related to discipline.

His sentence had been declared invalid within three days of 11 August, 1992. It was signed by the chairman of the Court Senate and carried the official stamp of the Military Court. It entitled my father to "rehabilitation" and financial compensation if he wished. These he refused.

The things of the fight still loosely surround my father. In his library, where the old mandolin sits, there is a book by Josef Macek inscribed to him during a Pittsburgh visit in 1956. In a drawer of his desk is a collection of correspondence from the nineteen-fifties with the Czech statesman, a sheath of onionskin paper heavily laid over with Czech type. In the same drawer, folded carefully, is a large Czech flag I brought him from my trip. On another shelf nearby there is a piece of the Berlin Wall that I gave him the year it came down.

For his seventieth birthday, in August of 1995, Mira flew to be with my father for the first time since the revolution. I picked her up at Logan airport in Boston, and we drove north together the following morning. She was still having trouble with her hip, but when she arrived at my parents' home she walked eagerly to the stairs that my father came down, saying, *Brácho*, brother. In the early autumn sun of America, my aunt and my father held one another.

I am haunted by the story I have come to these pages to tell. Throughout my writing, my father's voice has been with me, giving me a simple message that now I thoroughly understand. Serve the truth, he says: resist all trespass on the spirit.

I have a thought for him as well, and one morning in America, many months after my journey, I woke to write it as a last entry into my Czech notebook:
Father.

Your country is free now, and you were there to fight for it when other men would have run. So when you've finished reading my words, close your eyes, and think of this:

That high on a hill called Kalvárie, overlooking your childhood town of Radnice, the fields of light are stirring.

They are waiting for you to walk among them again.

Josef in Germany, 1954.

SELECTED
BIBLIOGRAPHY

Clapham, John. *Smetana*. New York: Octagon Books, 1972.

Havel, Václav. *Disturbing The Peace*. New York: Vintage, 1991.

——. *Open Letters*. New York: Knopf, 1991.

——. *Summer Meditations*. New York: Knopf, 1992.

——. *Toward a Civil Society*. Prague: Lidove Noviny, 1995.

Heymann, Frederick G. *John Žižka and the Hussite Revolution*. Princeton: Princeton University Press, 1955.

Hofer, Hans. *Insight Guides: Prague*. Boston: Houghton Mifflin Company, 1993.

Konas, Josef; Tregellas, John, and Sasková, Lucie. *Prague Legends*. Prague: Agropress, 1991.

Korbel, Josef. *The Communist Subversion of Czechoslovakia*. Princeton: Princeton University Press, 1959.

Kovtun, George J. *Tomáš G. Masaryk 1850–1937*. Washington: Library of Congress, 1981.

——, Ed. *The Spirit of Thomas G. Masaryk (1850–1937)* (anthology of Masaryk's writings), New York: St. Martin's Press, 1990.

Kriseová, Eda. *Václav Havel: The Authorized Biography*. New York: St. Martin's Press, 1993.

London, Artur. *The Confession*. New York: Ballantine Books, Inc., 1971.

Macek, Josef. *An Essay on the Impact of Marxism*. Pittsburgh: University of Pittsburgh Press, 1955.

MacDonald, Callum. *The Killing of SS Obergruppenführer Reinhard Heydrich*. New York: The Free Press/MacMillan Inc., 1989.

Payne, Robert. *The Life and Death of Adolf Hitler*. New York: Praeger Publishers, 1973.

Pynsent, Robert B., Ed. *T.G. Masaryk (1850–1937): Volume 2. Thinker and Critic*. New York: St. Martin's Press, 1989.

Rittlinger, Herbert. *Sjížděl Jsem Drave Reky*. Prague: Nakladatelstvi Orbis, 1942.

——. *Voda Kajak Stan*. Prague: Orbis, 1944.

Seton-Watson, R.W. *Masaryk In England*. New York: The MacMillan Company, 1943.

Shirer, William L. *The Rise and Fall of the Third Reich*. New York: Simon and Schuster, 1960.

Steed, Wickham. *Czechoslovakia: Land of Dream and Enterprise*. London: Czechoslovak Ministry of Foreign Affairs, 1945.

Soukup, Vladimír, et. al. *Prague*. New York: Dorling Kindersley, 1994.

Sterling, Claire. *The Masaryk Case*. New York: Harper & Row, Publishers, 1969.

Svandrlik, Miloslav. *Prague Ghosts*. Prague: CTK—
Pragopress, 1968.

Sviták, Ivan. *The Czechoslovak Experiment: 1968–
1969*. New York and London: Columbia University Press, 1971.

Svoboda, Alois. *Prague Guidebook*. Prague: Sportovni a Turisticke Nakladatelstvi, 1965.

Szulc, Tad. *Czechoslovakia Since World War II*. New York: The Viking Press, 1971.

Toland, John. *Adolf Hitler*. New York: Ballantine Books, 1976.

Wheaton, Bernard and Kavan, Zdeněk. *The Velvet Revolution*. Boulder, CO: Westview Press, 1992.

Zeman, Zdeněk. *The Masaryks: The Making of Czechoslovakia*. New York: Harper & Row Publishers, Inc., 1976.